How to Write Better Résumés

THIRD EDITION

by
Adele Lewis

Former President and Founder,
Career Blazers Agency, Inc.
New York City

BARRON'S

BARRON'S EDUCATIONAL SERIES, INC.
New York • London • Toronto • Sydney

All inquiries should be addressed to:
Barron's Educational Series, Inc.
250 Wireless Boulevard
Hauppauge, NY 11788

Library of Congress Catalog Card No. 89-6696

International Standard Book No. 0-8120-4271-9

Library of Congress Cataloging-in-Publication Data

Lewis, Adele Beatrice. 1927–
 How to write better résumés/by Adele Lewis.—3rd ed.
 p. cm.
 ISBN 0-8120-4271-9
 1. Résumés (Employment) I. Title.
HF5383.L48 1989
650.14—dc20
                                89-6696

PRINTED IN THE UNITED STATES OF AMERICA
 012 100 987654

Contents

Introduction

If you are reading these words in a bookstore or library, trying to decide whether this book is worth your time and money, let us help you decide. We assume that, having turned to this page, you are interested in improving or changing your position. We also assume you know that a powerful, effective résumé is one essential tool toward accomplishing that goal.

Probably you want to continue working in your current career area; or you are changing career fields but know precisely in what new area you want to apply past career interests, skills, and achievements. From these assumptions we frame our entire universe of prospective readers, and we welcome you among them. This book will show you how to apply your skills to finding the job that satisfies you most.

In looking for a job, you should always aim for the very best and try to avoid settling for less. Be sure, however, that you maintain an open and realistic attitude, evaluating each opportunity with a flexible, far-sighted view. It is also our belief that you should take the job where you'll be happiest. Every job has psychological fringe benefits, and these, in the long run, can more than counter what might be viewed as a slight initial salary deficiency. If you are happy in your job, you'll do better work (and conversely, if you do better work, you'll be happy). Soon you will receive tangible recognition of that work. The contentment in your work will spill out into other areas of your life and is, therefore, an important and vital job asset. May this book ultimately bring you happiness.

I wish to thank all our clients, both job seekers and recruiters, who were so generous with their time and their suggestions. I am very grateful to my son, William Lewis, President of Career Blazers Personnel Services, Inc., for his continual support and for keeping me supplied with an excellent staff of researchers and résumés. And, lastly, special thanks to Diane DeGeorgis for her continual patience in typing and retyping the manuscript.

The Art of Job Hunting

Whether you're unemployed, just starting out, or simply looking for greener pastures, your job hunt can be either a triumphant experience or a complete catastrophe. From my long experience with dealing with a variety of job seekers, I've come to realize there is a definite skill to the looking for and getting of jobs. For those lucky few who intuitively possess this skill, job hunting is an exhilarating, rewarding experience. Conversely, for those not possessing this skill, job hunting can be a depressing, traumatic task. Fortunately, this skill can be learned. It is rarely innate, never offered as part of any educational curriculum, and hardly ever recognized as an independent skill. It requires lots of thought, a dedication to assume new attitudes, self-discipline, and lots of perseverance before it can be mastered. Once acquired, it will stay with you for the rest of your life and serve as a tremendous source of security.

In looking for a job, you must always maintain a cheerful, optimistic attitude. Keep in mind, always, that you *will* get a job, and it really doesn't matter if it's this week or next month. When you consider that you spend more than 70,000 hours of your life on the job, doesn't it make sense to be generous with the time allotted to secure one?

Give up all negative myths relating to the job market: "It's not what you know; it's who you know," "No one over forty stands a chance of getting a good job," "You have to have the *exact* experience they're looking for," "They never hire anyone who's been fired," "Large employment gaps are the kiss of death," "It's impossible to change careers."

Anyone involved in recruiting will tell you that there is no validity to these beliefs. At Career Blazers, we are constantly placing people over forty in excellent positions in prestigious companies. We continually have job listings for persons interested in changing fields or careers. If it were true—"It's not what you know but who you know"—there would be no employment agencies, executive search firms, and no ads in the paper. Our placement files prove that "exact" experience is rarely a requirement. Employers are flexible, and although initially they might ask for certain qualifications, they tend to loose their rigidity and hire the person who best convinces them that he or she is right for the job.

People involved in hiring are relatively sophisticated; they don't automatically prejudge anyone who has been fired. They are aware that a person fired from a particular position at a different company might be extremely valuable to their company. They realize that since changing jobs is such a stressful experience, many people are willing to stay in intolerable situations rather than face the great unknown. Company A's loss may very likely be Company B's gain.

It is true that large gaps in employment history may require additional effort in job hunting. However, those people who remain confident and true to themselves as well as others will ultimately meet with success.

People are constantly changing careers. A person with a scientific background has excellent prospects for a career in technical sales. We've seen engineers become salespersons, teachers metamorphosed into publishers' reps, copywriters filling slots in marketing areas.

Looking for a job requires a great deal of effort, much insight, the necessity of developing a high frustration tolerance, and a strong determination not to become discouraged. Our vast experience in helping people find jobs tells us that discouragement is a luxury no job seeker can afford. This has become one of our favorite mottoes, and we believe every job seeker should incorporate it into his or her personal philosophy.

The Skill or Art of Job Hunting—A 4-Step Career Strategy

Step I is to first start your job hunt with a little research. Make sure your salary requirements are in line with those currently offered. The classified section of your local newspaper offers a wealth of such information. A few calls to appropriate search firms is another simple method of learning a great deal about market conditions.

You know exactly the kind of job you're looking for. You are qualified (both education and work history). And your salary expectations are realistic. You are well on your way.

Step II is your résumé. You know there are jobs available. You must now let the world know you are ready, willing, and available. You want to put your credentials on display and broadcast the fact that you are up for hire. Your résumé is the best possible vehicle for this information. It must look good, be easy to read and—most important—it must create interest in its product: You. To be successful, your résumé must totally and instantly convince the reader that you are, indeed, a person of substance and should be interviewed. Chapter 2 will show you in a logical, step-by-step approach just how this can be accomplished.

Step III follows with how to most effectively circulate your résumé. Chapter 5 gives you a crash course in cover letters that synergetically maximize the impact of your résumé. Chapter 6 discusses networking and job sources for effective career strategy.

Step IV is changing an interview into an offer. Chapter 8

discusses the skill of interviewing. We review the preparation necessary for successful interviewing, tell you how to handle multiple interviews, and give you proper techniques for salary negotiations. You'll learn how to control the interview and, finally how to convert that interview into a solid job offer. We are convinced that once these basic skills have been mastered, you will find job hunting to be a positive, uplifting experience.

Go for it!

Contents and Style of a Résumé 2

There was a time when job seekers could simply visit a potential employer and be interviewed, but that time has long since passed. In this complex world where distance, time, and sheer numbers mitigate against personal involvement, the résumé has become the most essential ingredient in both the job search and hiring process. As such, your résumé must represent you in the clearest, most forceful manner possible. It must represent you when you are not there to speak for yourself. In essence, your résumé becomes an embodiment of you, and will serve as your representative. The success of your job campaign is completely dependent on the effectiveness of your résumé. A good résumé results in interviews; an inferior one is simply discarded.

Employers tell us it is not unusual for them to receive hundreds of résumés each day. Under these circumstances, no more than ten or twenty seconds is given to scan each résumé before allowing time for a thorough read-through. If a résumé is more than two pages long, it will be immediately rejected, as will those that appear cluttered and don't invite easy reading. Spelling or grammatical mistakes are never tolerated. In order to warrant a thorough read-through, your résumé must show *immediately* that you have the ability to organize information and present it in a clear, concise manner. You must instantly communicate to the reader that you know where you are going with your career, and that you have just the right background to make you a valuable staff addition.

But let's begin with the basics. Every résumé must identify and describe the writer. It must include:

- Your name, address, and telephone number
- A description of your educational history
- A description of your work history
- Work-related honors or citations
- Publications, if any

It **may** also include:

- Your job objective or career goal
- A capsule description of your work history
- Memberships in any professional organizations
- Foreign languages you may know
- Information on hobbies, especially if they relate in some way or show diversity of interests
- Military service, if any
- Security clearance, if any (technical sales)

- Willingness to travel or relocate

It should **not** include the following information

- Reasons for leaving past jobs
- Past salaries or present salary requirements
- Personal data—age, height, weight, marital status, number of children
- Health status
- Names of spouse or children
- A photograph of yourself
- Names and addresses of references

Résumé Styles

Although every résumé should contain a brief, concise summary of your work history and educational background, the style or approach differs in the arrangement of this data. Though there are several résumé styles we believe the chronological is the most effective, and we strongly recommend that you choose this approach in writing your résumé. We will, however, discuss others as well and evaluate each style.

Despite minor variations, there are basically four different résumé styles or approaches.

- Chronological (Historical)
- Functional
- Synoptic/Amplified
- Imaginative, Creative, or Informal

We'll discuss each, with consideration of their usefulness.

The Chronological (Historical) Résumé

As the name applies, this style presents the information in chronological sequence. The succession of facts must be presented in **reverse** chronological order, starting with the present or most recent experience and moving backward in time.

As with any résumé, start with your name, addresss, and phone number. It is traditional in some industries to list your education first. There are no hard and fast rules about this, and certainly if you have a good, solid background of experience but have not completed your degree, then it makes sense to place the education at the end of the résumé instead. Usually, however, your most advanced degree is shown first, followed in reverse order by all other degrees. Again dates should always be used. State the name of the university, city, state, degree earned, and the dates attended. Academic honors would be included in this grouping.

If you have opted to use a career objective or résumé capsule, place it near the top of the first page. Keep it brief and realistic.

Your work history should list each job (in reverse chronological order), specifying your job title, the name of your employer, the address (city and state; number and name of street are not necessary) and a summary of your duties and responsibilities. These summaries should be brief but specific. Always include dates; they can be in vertical columns to the left of the other information, on a line before the description of each job held, or included as an integral part of the paragraph. Generally, placing the dates in a vertical column is preferable, as employers like to be able to determine at a glance the times involved.

The chronological résumé should be brief and take no more than two pages. This type of résumé offers a clear, concise picture of you, and it is probably the easiest to assimilate in a quick reading. Without exception, the chronological format was preferred by the corporate executives we've talked to; they felt it does the best job of indicating an individual's direction, background, accomplishments, and general qualifications.

The Functional Résumé

As its name implies, the functional résumé emphasizes the writer's qualifications and abilities. This approach rejects a chronological sequence of employment and educational history, and instead provides analyses of particular professional strengths. The employment strengths or skills are the important facts in this style of résumé.

Your work history, volunteer experience, and educational record are fragmented into significant talents, and each skill is listed separately. Because these functions or responsibilities usually have crossed over a number of jobs, the sequence of job history has been sacrificed to emphasize ability. Names of employers and dates are omitted from this section of the résumé, since the expertise has been gained from more than one position.

The functional résumé should be brief, concise, and well structured. It should start with your name, address, and phone number, your job objective, and a résumé summary (if needed). The body of the résumé should consist of four or five paragraphs, each one heading a particular area of expertise or involvement.

The skills paragraphs should be listed in order of importance. We define the most important skill as the function that is most similar to your present career goal or job objective.

Typical headings might be Marketing, Legal Secretarial,

Research, Sales Management, and so on. A brief summary of your accomplishments in each category would follow.

Though this type of résumé has gained in popularity over the past few years, very few employers, personnel men and women, and staff managers approve of this approach. Our employment experts tell us that they become very suspicious of the functional résumé. They feel it is often used to cover up a spotty work record (for example, seven jobs in four years or a long period of unemployment), to exaggerate certain abilities, or to disguise some "whole truth." One corporate executive put it succinctly when he said, "It raises more questions than it answers."

The only situation that lends itself to the functional résumé is one in which you are attempting a career change. In that case, this style résumé may be advantageous because it shows in a glance the kinds of jobs within your capacity. Because most résumé readers feel that résumés lose their effectiveness if dates or names of employers are not shown, you should overcome this by adding a very concise historical (always in reverse chronological order) listing of employers, job titles, and job descriptions with the appropriate dates. This history should follow your description by function.

The Synoptic/Amplified Résumé

The synoptic/amplified résumé is weak because, by definition, it requires the use of two or more pages and hence important information can be easily overlooked. The word *synoptic* means "affording a general view of a whole" while to *amplify* is to expand (as in statement) by the use of detail or illustration or by closer analysis. As the name suggests, this résumé gives both a general overview or simplification of your background as well as an expansive, detailed description.

The first page consists of all pertinent data such as name, address, and telephone number, plus résumé capsule, job objective (if included), employment history (with job titles and names and addresses of employuers) and dates of employment. Educational background is also included on the first page, and the entire history is arranged in reverse chronological order.

The succeeding pages repeat the employment history, but the job record is expanded or "amplified" to include a short narration describing the duties or responsibilities for each position held. This résumé is most effective if the duties and responsibilities encompass more than the job title implies, or if the work experience has been a long and varied one.

Although we see this style of résumé often, we do not recommend its use. The main disadvantage is that it may run on for several pages, taxing the reader's patience and taking too much of his time. Our corporate résumé readers tell us this style implies a certain arrogance and feeling of self-importance. With any résumé of more than two pages you take a chance on missing a thorough read-through, and with each additional page there also comes the increasing possibility of loss of a page, in effect, nullifying the impact of your résumé.

The Imaginative/Creative Résumé

You may feel that an imaginative, highly unusual approach is the ideal thing to shake loose your résumé from the pack. Using artwork, illustrations, cartoons, or a unique format may very well create an impression, but not necessarily a good one.

We have received résumés that were over two feet long, wound up like a scroll; very, very small ones put together to resemble a passport (the print so reduced you would have to use a magnifying glass, *if* you wanted to read it); résumés in the format of menus, playbills, calendars, stock certificates, and even a summons. True, these résumés caught the eye. They amused and charmed us, but they did not sustain enough interest to become effective. Such résumés are usually difficult to read, unprofessional, and impossible to file. Corporate employers share our opinion that a résumé is a business matter and, accordingly, should be presented in a businesslike, professional manner.

Putting Yourself on Paper

3

When preparing your résumé, always keep in mind the purpose of that résumé—to serve as a personal advertisement, generating enough interest in you to secure an interview. As an effective advertisement, it should be attractive, easy to read, concise, and informative. Because the chronological résumé is the most preferred style, we will use this approach in showing you how to write your résumé.

The information contained in the résumé should be presented in the following order:

- Identifying information
- Summary or résumé capsule (optional)
- Career or job objective (optional)
- Employment history
- Educational history
- Honors or citations, if any
- Publications, if any
- Membership in professional organizations (optional)

Including mention of military service, knowledge of foreign languages, hobbies, a willingness to travel or relocate, and other personal information is also optional, and there is no prescribed order. However, this information should appear near the end of the résumé.

In deciding whether to include a job objective and/or a job summary, consider that your present or most recent job description should be on the first page. If your objective and/or summary are too long, it may be better to shorten both or omit one of them.

Identifying Information

Always start with your identifying material in a conspicuous position, either flush left (leaving room for the margin) or on the top center (again leave about ¾ to 1½ inches for the margin). Give your complete name, street address, city, state, zip code and phone number, complete with area code. If you can be reached at the office, that number should also be listed.

The use of the summary, also called a résumé capsule, is optional, and mainly used by condidates with a least five years of experience. To be effective, it must include information indicating that you are indeed qualified for the position sought. Although optional, we have been told by more than one personnel director of an important company that this is the first piece of information they scan. If the summary, essentially a digest of the résumé, sustains their interest, they will continue and read the résumé in its entirety. The beauty of the summary is that it gives you the power of the functional résumé and, at the same time, excludes all of its disadvantages. Here is your opportunity to combine and build on similar aspects of your background that may have been acquired over a period of many years in a number of different positions.

Suppose one of your accomplishments occurred in an early job. If you were using a straight reverse-chronological style presentation, this important information might not be noticed by the reader. It probably would appear near the bottom of the page or possibly on the second page, and would very likely be missed. The summary allows you to emphasize it at the beginning. It is the space where you can list the highlights or whatever else you might consider your biggest career accomplishment, regardless of when that was.

The summary should consist of one strong sentence, three or four at the most. Those sentences should be enough to highlight the aspects of your background that will most appeal to a potential employer.

Here are some samples of summary paraagraphs:

> "Seventeen years of sales growth achievement in the medical field, having established strong rapport with professional practitioners."

> "More than 12 years involvement in the C language, UNIX area of programming both in Systems and Applications. Thoroughly experienced in designing, implementing, and debugging."

> "Fifteen years experience in Nuclear Power Plant Engineering, including start-up, modifications, construction, installation, and testing of ASME Code Class I, II, and III Systems."

We suggest that you write down every skill, responsibility, job duty, and accomplishment that will qualify you for your next position. Think of every problem you had some part in solving, any new idea you contributed to which was ultimately used by your employer, any achievements or capabiltiies you have which would demonstrate or suggest that you can do the job better than anyone else.

Study your list, and pare it down to five or six points. Combine those that are similar in function so that you can write a brief narrative that has a convincing tone to it. Be brief. Choose your words carefully.

You may have to write several drafts—shortening sentences,

changing a word here and there, deleting unnecessary adjectives or phrases that might be repetitive. Work on it until you have it perfect.

The summary or capsule résumé is the best way of emphasizing solid work background and highlighting specific qualifications to a targeted employer. Although it often involves retyping the résumé for each potential employer, the capsule résumé can be the only part of your résumé that does have to be adjusted to suit different employer's needs.

Job Objective or Career Goal

As with the summary, the use of a job objective or career goal is strictly optional. It is usually used when an individual has background in more than one area and has preference in a particular direction.

We've seen excellent results with résumés that include objectives as well as those that omit this information. The purpose of the objective is to describe succinctly the position you want by job title, function, and/or industry. The job objective must logically connect with the balance of your résumé. The contents of your résumé must demonstrate that you are indeed qualified for the position you are seeking. You should avoid stating objectives that are too confining; you don't want to cancel out opportunities that might be of interest to you. On the other hand, be careful of clichés ("a position that is both rewarding and stimulating") ("a challenging position which offers growth potential"). Such statements are meaningless and the reader may infer you either lack direction or are unsure of what your career goals are. The following are examples.

> "A position with management potential in the system software area in a technically advanced environment."

> "Seeking corporate position where my expertise in editorial design will be employed in communications media for both external and internal circulation."

Employment History

The heart of your résumé is the section that describes your experience or employment history. It is important to remember that your résumé must be honest as well as logical. Never put anything in your résumé that is not 100 percent true. Stay with the truth, even if you feel a small exaggeration or distortion might make you more marketable. Any information that is not true can become an insurmountable liability. Employers usually expect that a new employee will require some training, and they are quite willing to do so. If, however, you claimed certain strengths and are unable to demonstrate those abilities, you can be sure your credibility on all other matters will be questioned.

Begin your employment history with your present or most recent experience. Work backwards, treating each position as an independent entry. Each job mentioned should include the name and address (city and state; no streets or numbers) of the employer, the dates involved (month and year), and a concise description of your responsibilities. If you are presently employed, use the present tense in describing your current position and, obviously, the past tense for former jobs. Use only implied pronouns in crisp, simple language. Writing in the third person (he/she) is stylistically objectionable, as well as suggesting a certain detachment. Using the first person (I) is redundant; plainly the person reading the résumé is aware that you are the subject of your own résumé. For example, compare the following "bits" of information:

> "She/he was responsible for creation of marketing concepts"

> "I was responsible for creation of marketing concepts"

> "Responsible for creation of marketing concepts"

Always give the name of each company you have worked for, including your present employer, even though you may wish this to be considered confidential. You will weaken your résumé by not including specific names. Once we received a résumé without any company identifying information, and decided we were not interested in that candidate. Luckily, he followed up with a phone call. It was only when he told us the name of the company, which happened to be a direct competitor, that we realized his experience was exactly what we were looking for. It is understandable that you might be circumspect about the fact that you are looking for a job. However, all agencies and employers treat this information as confidential.

Your goal in this section of the résumé is to make as much as you can of each postion you have had, while keeping the descriptions as brief as possible. Describe your major responsibilities while concentrating heavily on the accomplishments you can legitimately own or share.

Always be as specific as possible and avoid generalities or long descriptions of the company you worked for. Describe exactly what you did and what your responsibilities were.

Think of as many problems as you can that faced you and you were able to solve. Our questionnaire on page 21 will help you to organize these thoughts. Mention any improvements you were responsible for, any ideas adopted by your employer. Describe actions you took to solve problems and the positive conditions that were the consequences of your efforts. Don't be shy; never be humble. But never be arrogant, either. Be proud of your achievements.

The job descriptions should be just that and, although it is important to list accomplishments, it also has to paint an accurate picture of what your daily routine included.

You may assume that an interviewer's interest will be piqued by each of your employment history entries, and you will be asked to elaborate on them in the interview. View each bit of information you provide as the basis of a future leading question. It's a good idea to mentally rehearse your responses as you write your job description.

Use active verbs; they give a certain power to your résumé. And choose your words carefully; make each word count. Avoid being flowery; too many adjectives, especially an overabundance of superlatives, lessens the impact of your résumé.

Keep in mind, always, that you're aiming for a 1–2-page résumé. Be brief, concise. Keep narratives describing each position succinct—no more than five to ten lines. Each accomplishment should be broken up into bite-sized entities for the reader to spot and digest quickly. Information concerning past positions should **not** be as long as current or recent ones. Avoid repetition—if your job responsibilities were similar in more than one job, describe in detail only the most recent position. Also, it is not necessary to use complete sentences. Indent and use "banner" statements to emphasize accomplishments. Start such entries with an asterisk (*) or dot (•) so they appear to "pop" out.

Rewrite your first draft. It may be necessary to rewrite it several times, striking out unnecessary words and phrases and tightening sentences until they say exactly what you mean. Reread it several times, checking for spelling and grammatical errors. After several rereadings, have a friend or colleague scan it. Another person may pick up errors that you have missed and possibly suggest some additional qualifications.

Educational History

Start with your most advanced degree and include the name and location of the college or university you attended, the degrees you earned, and the year you graduated. Mention your major field of study and all career-oriented scholarships and academic awards. Thereafter, list—in reverse chronological order—all other degrees until you reach your B.A. or B.S. Include the same information for each as described for the advanced degree. Though abbreviations generally should not be used in résumés, it is acceptable and correct in listing your degrees; for example, Ph.D., M.S., B.A., B.S. If you have attended college, it is not necessary to include information concerning high school.

A recent graduate should mention his or her grade point average if it is 3.5 or higher. Obviously, there is no point in calling attention to a C average. If you were Phi Beta Kappa, Summa, or Magna Cum Laude, or if you received other high academic honors, no matter what level of experience you have, by all means mention it.

Professional Societies and Publications

List all professional associations and organizations that are career related. Your membership in such groups implies dedication to your field and an ability to get along with others. If you are or have ever been an officer in any organization, be sure to mention that fact.

Personal Information

Remember a very simple rule: *Personal information should never be included in your résumé.* (Though earlier editions of this book told you that such information as your height, weight, marital status, and number of children was optional, times have changed.)

Your résumé should include only information describing your qualifications; any other information is considered inappropriate and unprofessional.

Because the passage of employment laws have made it illegal for an employer to question an individual as to his or her age, sex, race, or religious preference, such information does *not* belong on a résumé.

Your state of health (it's always "excellent" anyway) is superfluous. If, however, you have a disability and feel you want the potential employer to know about it before the interview, mention it in your covering letter, *not* in the résumé. Bear in mind that your résumé should emphasize your *abilities*, not your disabilities.

Should you include your hobbies and leisure-time activities? Again, the answer is *no*. It simply is not necessary. Keep in mind that every word in your résumé should be there for a reason and there is no purpose to a description of your nonprofessional or work-related interests.

References

Never, never supply the names of your references on your résumé. Not only is it unprofessional, but it can cause a lot of bother to those individuals listed. Simply state, as the last entry on your résumé, "References on Request" or "References will be furnished upon request."

Always get permission from those individuals you wish to use as references. Don't put yourself or them in the position in which any calls about you will come as a surprise to them. Try, if possible, to get references that can be reached quickly. For that reason, it is preferable to list persons who can be reached by phone rather than by mail. Make certain you have all of their current addresses and phone numbers. If you are giving a person's business phone, check to see if he or she is still employed by the same company.

If your name has been changed through marriage or for any other reason during your work or educational history, be sure that your references know you by your new name. It is wise for women who have married and have adopted their husband's name to indicate their maiden name as well. Lastly, you should give permission to call your references only when an employer has indicated that you are under serious consideration.

Photographs

Never! Never, unless you are looking for a job as a model/salesperson "whatever!" Not only are photographs on résumés unprofessional, but their legality is questionable. If an employer kept résumés containing photographs on file, that action could be considered a covert form of racial, sex, or age screening and, as such, could be considered illegal. But more important to you, don't prejudice your chances by sending a photo.

Reasons For Leaving Past Jobs

An emphatic NO! Your résumé should be a businesslike summary of your talents, qualifications, goals, work history, and education. Since the reasons you left previous employers do not add to that summary, they should not be included in your résumé.

Salaries, Past and Present

Salaries—neither your present minimum nor your past earnings—should be discussed or listed in your résumé. A potential employer will probably arrange a series of interviews, and the subject of salary will most often be discussed close to or at the final meeting.

Every employer we've had contact with considers salary a most confidential matter. It is considered extremely unprofessional as well as indiscreet for employees to discuss salaries among themselves. Your résumé will be seen by many individuals in the company who normally would not and **should not** know your salary range, so no indication of it should appear in your résumé.

Should you at least include your salary requirement? No. Including your salary requirements might eliminate you from certain positions in which the remuneration has not yet been decided; or it might preclude you from obtaining a certain position with an already-established higher salary. As we've indicated before, reserve your discussion of salary for the final interview.

Résumé Appearance

Visualize an employer who, after placing an ad, receives over two hundred résumés. He or she is also developing new systems, planning programs, and has a desk filled with other projects demanding attention. He or she is now faced with selecting the résumés to read more closely. Obviously, the first step is to scan. As we've mentioned earlier, our inquiries have shown that an average recruiter rarely gives more than ten seconds attention to a résumé in deciding whether it merits a complete reading.

Put yourself in the reader's position. Do you actually read every word in every newspaper or magazine you look at? We're sure your answer is in the negative. In this fast-paced world, who has the time or even the interest? Rather, you automatically scan the material to decide which articles, advertisements, or stories are worth your time for a thorough read-through. The print media has proved that "eye appeal" is as important as content; people simply discard that which is difficult to read. And we are aware that many staff managers and employers discard résumés containing excellent material because they were poorly presented. Remember—your résumé, to do its job, must pass the "quick scan test."

To pass this test, your résumé must be visually inviting. Start by selecting a format. You will find some samples that have been successful beginning on page 28. Whether you choose one of these samples or create your own, be sure that the total effect is pleasing to the eye. Be equally sure that it is easy to read, and that the different sections are clearly separated from one another.

Separate thoughts into paragraphs with pleasing white space

between them. There is nothing more difficult to scan than a long, solid block of text, with no breaks or indentations. Even better, itemize and highlight thoughts with dashes or asterisks. At the very least, separate each job by white space, providing different sections to the résumé.

Use good-quality paper and a clear, dark typewriter ribbon or cartridge. Make sure your typewriter's keys are clean, assuring you a clean, crisp copy. If you decide to use a paper color other than white, be sure it is a pastel that will contrast well with the color of your type. (Beige paper with dark brown type is quite effective.) Avoid vibrant, or otherwise off-beat colors.

Use standard 8½ by 11-inch bond paper. It is a professional size, is easily handled, and is convenient to file. Avoid legal size paper, plastic sheet covers, or report folders—again, all too difficult to file. Keep away from unprofessional visual effects; photographs, illustrations, wild formats, or too many mixed-type styles.

Aim for one or two pages of typewritten material. Use only one side of the paper, and if the résumé is more than one page, staple the pages together, being sure that your name appears on each page.

Giving Your Résumé "Eye Appeal"

A professional layout should be subtle and unobtrusive, but at the same time it should direct the reader's eye to the most important information. You can accomplish this by using proper width margins, combining upper and lower case, underlining special items, as well as enclosing the entire résumé in a penned-in-border.

Use the ground—the white space on your paper—effectively. Use your margins imaginatively; use wide margins to lend importance to the information on the page and, at the same time, to provide a restful, easy-on-the-eye appearance. Create white space by double or triple spacing between blocks of information.

Be selective in your use of upper case; perhaps reserve it for job titles or names of employers. You might underline major accomplishments, but this, too, should be done sparingly. Avoid allowing your résumé to look too "busy," which is often what results when you use too many type faces and a plethora of underlines.

Reproduction

There was a time when employers expected every résumé to be individually typed. Fortunately, those days have passed. Although carbon or mimeograph copies are not acceptable (because of smudging and lack of clarity), any other duplicating process that turns out clear, sharp copies may be used.

Photocopying and offset printing give excellent results. Even Xerox copies are acceptable as long as they are sharp and clear. Offset printing should cost no more than a few dollars per one hundred copies, a relatively small price to pay for a crisp, professional-looking résumé.

Since the success of your job campaign very likely may hinge upon the appearance of your résumé, it is important that you have a superior product. Printing and copying services are listed in the telephone yellow pages under the heading "Offset Reproduction." Many of these services will also be able to retype your résumé and assist you with the layout and choice of available type faces.

Organizing Your Thoughts

Before you sit down to actually write your résumé, it is imperative that you organize all your information in terms of dates, education and courses, employers, job responsibilities, and all the other data that will be included. We've found that the most difficult part of writing a résumé is putting your thoughts and data into a meaningful form. To help you accomplish this, we have provided a series of workspaces: forms and worksheets that will force you to analyze your data and organize it to correspond with the standard résumé formats. Using these worksheets will force you to examine the natures of your previous jobs and your particular skills and strengths, and will pay off tremendously later on when you begin writing your résumé and when you have your job interviews. This chapter actually becomes a skeleton version of the first draft of your résumé.

Résumé Workspace

Use the space that follows to provide the information indicated.

Identifying Information

Complete the following information.

Name:_____
      (If married woman, include married and maiden names.)

Address:_____
      (Street and number, city, state, and zip code.)

Home Phone:_____
      (Be sure to give area code.)

Business Phone:_____
      (Be sure to give area code.)

Note: If your business phone is confidential, state that, for example:
      Business phone: (212) 555-1280 (confidential)

Résumé Capsule

The résumé capsule, as with the job objective, is an optional feature. However, one or the other must be used if you are trying to change careers. Use this space to write a résumé capsule, whether you decide to use it on your final résumé or not.

_____

_____

_____

_____

_____

_____

_____

Job Objective

Remember, the job objective is **optional.** If used, keep it brief. The only time it **must** be used is if you are trying to change careers.

_____

_____

_____

_____

Employment History

Your employment history should be listed in **reverse chronological order.**

Name of Company:_____

Address of Company:_____

_____

_____

Job Title:_____

Dates: Description of Responsibilities:_____

From   To
(Month/Year) (Month/Year)

_____ _____   _____

_____

_____

Name of Company: _____

Address of Company: _____

_____

_____

Job Title: _____

Dates:

From   **To**

(Month/Year)   (Month/Year)

_____   _____

Description of Responsibilities: _____

_____

_____

_____

_____

_____

_____

Name of Company: _____

Address of Company: _____

_____

_____

Job Title: _____

Dates:

From   **To**

(Month/Year)   (Month/Year)

_____   _____

Description of Responsibilities: _____

_____

_____

_____

_____

_____

_____

Educational History

List your education as you did your employment history, **in reverse chronological order**: your most advanced degree or your most recent education is first. Be sure to list all pertinent details—dates, degrees earned, educational institutions attended, and so on.

Advanced Degree
Dates:

From   To
(year)   (year)

_____
(Name of university)

_____   _____

_____
(Address of university)

Undergraduate Degree
Dates:

_____
(Degrees or credits earned)

From   To
(year)   (year)

_____
(Name of university)

_____   _____

_____
(Address of university)

_____
(Degree or credits earned)

_____
(Major)   (Minor)

Personal Information

Publications and Major Achievements:_____

_____

_____

Foreign Languages or any other special skills:_____

_____

Associations

_____

_____

_____

_____

_____

References

Though the names of your references should **never** be included on your résumé, it is a good idea to assemble your data at the time you are preparing your résumé. Have a minimum of three people as references. It is advisable to include a statement that references will be furnished upon request.

Note: List the complete address—street and number, city, state, and zip code. Give area code with telephone number.

Name of Reference:_____

Position:_____

Company Affiliation:_____

Company Address:_____

_____

Business Phone and Extension:_____

Name of Reference:_____

Position:_____

Company Affiliation:_____

Company Address:_____

_____

Business Phone and Extension:_____

Name of Reference:_____

Position:_____

Company Affiliation:_____

Company Address:_____

_____

Business Phone and Extension:_____

Name of Reference:_____

Position:_____

Company Affiliation:_____

Company Address:_____

_____

Business Phone and Extension:_____

Action Words

Linked up with identifying your responsiblities and portraying your previous jobs is the matter of using strong, descriptive words to describe those activities. Look over the list of words below to help you identify ones that reflect or describe your job responsibilities and/or accomplishments. Use these words as needed to complete the Employment History Worksheets.

A— accomplish, account, accumulate, acquire, activate, adhere, administer, advertise, advise, allocate, analyze, appraise, approve, arrange, assign, assist, assume, assure, audit, augment, authorize, automate

B— brought, budget, built

C— catalog, change, code, collect, communicate, compare, compile, complete, compose, compute, conceive, concentrate, conduct, configure, consider, construct, consult, continue, contract, contribute, control, cooperate, coordinate, correct, correlate, create, credit

D— debug, decrease, define, delegate, delete, design, determine, develop, direct, disperse, display, distribute, document

E— edit, educate, emphasize, employ, engage, engineer, enhance, enlarge, ensure, establish, examine, execute, exercise, expand, expedite, extend, evaluate

F— fix, flowchart, forecast, function as, furnish

G— generate, grant, graph, guarantee

H— head, help, hire

I— implement, improve, include, increase, inform, initialize, initiate, inspect, install, instruct, integrate, interfere, interpret, interview, invent, investigate, involve, issue

J— join, justify

L— lease, lessen, load

M— maintain, manage, market, master, measure, meet, modify, monitor, motivate

N— negotiate, neutralize, normalize, notify

O— open, operate, orchestrate, order, organize

P— participate, perform, persuade, plan, post, prepare, present, process, procure, produce, program, project, promote, propose, protect, provide, publicize, purchase

Q— qualify, quantify

R— reclaim, recommend, reconstruct, recruit, release, report, represent, request, require, requisition, research, reshape, responsible for, retain, retrieve, review, revise

S— schedule, screen, secure, select, sell, serve, set objectives, set up, solve, sort, specify, staff, standardize, stimulate, strenghten, structure, subcontract, submit, succeed, summarize, supervise, supply, support, synthesize, systematize

T— teach, test, trace, track, train, transfer, translate

U— update, upgrade, underscore, utilize

V— validate, verify, visualize

W—write

Sample Layouts

Name
Street Address
City, State, Zip Code

Home Phone #
Business Phone #

Employment History

Job Title

From (date)
To present

Name of Company
Address of Company

Write out duties and responsibilities of job in question.

Job Title

From (date)
To (date)

Name of Company
Address of Company

Write out duties and responsibilities of job in question.

Job Title

From (date)
To (date)

Name of Company
Address of Company

Write out duties and responsibilities of job in question.

Educational History

From (date)
To (date)

Name of College
Address of College
Degree Earned

References: On Request

Name
Street Address
City, State, Zip Code
Home Phone #
Business Phone #

Employment History

Job Title

From (date)   Name of Company
To present   Address of Company

                               Duties and responsibilities of job written out.

Job Title

From (date)   Name of Company
To (date)   Address of Company

                               Duties and responsibilities.

Educational History

From (date)   Name of College
To (date)   Address of College
                               Graduate Degree

From (date)   Name of College
To (date)   Address of College
                               Undergraduate Degree

References: Available on Request

Résumé of Qualifications

Name
Street Address
City, State, Zip Code
Home Phone #
Business Phone #

<u>Career Objective</u>

To use the experience gained in . . .

<u>Educational History</u>

Name of College   From (date)
Address of College   To (date)
Advanced Degree

Name of College   From (date)
Address of College   To (date)
Bachelor's Degree

<u>Employment History</u>

<u>Job Title</u>

Name of Company   From (date)
Address of Company   To present

Description of duties and responsibilities in the above company.

<u>Job Title</u>

Name of Company   From (date)
Address of Company   To (date)

Description of duties and responsibilities in the company mentioned above.

<u>Job Title</u>

Name of Company   From (date)
Address of Company   To (date)

Description of duties and responsibilities.

<u>References:</u>   Available on Request

Resume of _____ *(name)* _____

Street Address
City, State, Zip Code
Home Phone #
Business Phone #

Employment History

Job Title
Name and Address of Company

Description of job, giving duties and responsibilities.

From (date) to present

Job Title
Name and Address of Company

Description of job.

From (date) to (date)

Educational History

Name and Address of College
Degree Received

From (date) to (date)

References: Available on Request

Resume of:

Name

Street Address
City, State, Zip Code

Home Phone #
Business Phone #

Career Objective   To work as a ...

Employment History

From (date)   Job Title — Name of Company
To present   Address of Company

Description of duties and responsibilities in this job.

From (date)   Job Title — Name of Company
To (date)   Address of Company

Description of responsibilities and duties in this position.

From (date)   Job Title — Name of Company
To (date)   Address of Company

Description of nature of employment with duties and responsibilities.

Educational History   Degree — Name of College
                                       Address of College

References   Furnished on Request

The Cover Letter

A cover letter should be enclosed every time you send out your résumé. Its enclosure is not only an act of courtesy but a means of adding a personal touch. It gives each individual you approach an indication of your personal attention to his or her situation—which would not be the case if the résumé arrived unaccompanied. The cover letter also neutralizes the tone of the impersonal, reproduced résumé.

This is your chance to let your individual style, personality, and unique strengths stand out from the crowd. Don't be afraid to "sell" yourself here by describing some unique incident or experience. If you wish to do something flamboyant, the cover letter, rather than the résumé, is the place to do it.

Our corporate experts tell us they are much more likely to read a résumé accompanied by a covering letter than one received without a letter. The letter removes the look of a mass mailing.

It doesn't matter whether you are sending your résumé in answer to an ad, to an employment agency, or as part of your personal mailing campaign. The cover letter will always follow the same, simple rules. It should be brief—limited to one page and no more than four paragraphs. Needless to say, it should be neatly typed, and conform to the standards of business correspondence.

Whenever possible, address the letter to a particular individual in the company, preferably by name and title. If it is impossible to ascertain the name, address the letter to "Personnel Director" or, by title, to the head of the department in which you are hoping to work. In answering an ad, however, address your letter as the ad indicates. If there is no more than a box number, simply address it to that box number.

The first paragraph of your letter is the most important, since it may determine whether or not the reader continues to read. Just as in a newspaper article, the first sentence or "lead" should be original and informative, and it should set the tone for the rest of the letter. It should tell why you are writing to that particular person or company. If it is in answer to an ad, say so, and give the name and date of the publication where the ad appeared. If the letter is part of your direct mail campaign, explain in two or three lines either why you would like to work for that particular company or why you feel their hiring you would be in their company's best interest. A frequent mistake in cover letters is to describe why the job is in the candidate's best interest, rather than to stress what the candidate can do for the employer. For example, to say "I believe your firm can offer me the dynamic challenges and responsibilities I seek" does not convince a recruiter of what you have to offer that company.

If a friend who is an employee has suggested you make contact with this particular company, you should give the name, title or job category, and the department where the friend is employed.

Some typical opening lines are:

> "Dorothy Johnson, a programmer in the systems programming department, suggested that I write to you."

> "I am replying to your ad which appeared in the New York *Times* on Sunday, May 12th."

> "Your recent acquisition of Zebulon Textiles Company led me to believe that you might be interested in my nine years experience as a marketing manager with extensive industry experience."

The following one or two paragraphs should point out the salient features of your résumé which could be of interest to your correspondent. These paragraphs are the very guts of your covering letter. In a sentence or two, tell why you would be an asset to the company receiving your letter. Succinctly lay out your credentials, and refer to your accomplishments, skills, or areas of expertise. In certain circumstances, you might elaborate on one or two entries on your résumé.

Use the cover letter to describe special projects in which you played a key role, or the features of a program you worked on which were unusual. Another frequent use of the cover letter is to summarize your achievements in a somewhat more readable form than the optional summary portion of the résumé.

Because different aspects of your résumé are highlighted in each cover letter, the same résumé can be used to pursue different job opportunities. The covering letter, stressing your most appropriate skills and talents, can be geared uniquely to each particular company that will be the recipient of your résumé.

The last paragraph should be the closing, indicating your hope that you have created interest in yourself, your wish to thank the reader for his or her consideration, and your suggestion that you will call shortly to arrange an interview. Unless you are replying to a box number ad, always state that you will initiate the action to obtain an interview.

Taking the initiative is important. Saying you will call to set up a date for the interview increases your chances of getting it. Essential as it is for employers to recruit the best people, the press of day-to-day responsibilities often pushes this need down the list of professional priorities. Because enough candidates will call to set up interviews, it is very likely the job will be filled before the employer can take the necessary action to set up a series of appointments.

Types of Cover Letters

There are several situations that require you to mail your résumé and cover letter. These are:

- A response to an ad.
- An unsolicited inquiry to a targeted employer as part of your direct mail campaign.
- A letter to an employment agency.
- A letter to a friend or colleague who might offer assistance in a job search.

Response to an Ad

Read the ads carefully, marking or clipping those of interest to you. Examine the requirements thoroughly. Employers advertise for the "ideal" candidate and, more often than not, actually hire an individual not possessing every qualification listed in the original ad. For that reason, it is a good idea to reply not only to those ads which fit you perfectly, but also to those for which you meet just some of the requirements.

Now reread each ad you intend to answer. Study each separately. Assume that the requirements are rank ordered, and deal with each as sequenced in the ad. List on a piece of scratch paper every qualification, skill, strength, or accomplishment you possess relevant to the particular advertisement. If you don't have all the requirements, make a note of any experience in either your education or work history that demonstrates other capabilities which would make you an asset to that particular company. Write and rewrite this information until you have eliminated all excess words. Communicate your strengths clearly and succinctly. Work on your letter until each idea flows effortlessly to the next. Let's look at a typical ad and consider how to respond to it.

SALES MANAGER/TRAVEL

Famous-brand "Last Ever" sporting goods offers excellent opportunity. Territory includes N.Y., Mass., Vt., N.H., Me. Must have previous sales and travel experience. Salary, commission, bonus. Car & travel expenses plus complete benefits. Write Box 6214.

An appropriate reply can be found on page 39. Address your letter to the company and person listed in the ad, or simply to the Personnel Director if no individual's name is listed.

It's a good idea to research each company whose ad you intend to answer, and then include in your letter any new information you have become aware of: an expansion, recent or imminent merger, acquisition, or new product developments or services. Mention how you would be able to help the organization implement or maximize its current goals. (Obviously, if the ad lists only a box number, this will not be possible.)

Don't be discouraged if you don't get an immediate repsonse. We've found it is not unusual for a recruiter to hold résumés for more than six weeks before setting up interviews.

An effective method of making certain your résumé will be noticed is to write your cover letter in the form of a mailgram. This guarantees a certain exclusivity, expecially when answering an ad which is likely to attract a plethora of résumés. This is one situation where you must not be shy. Don't be afraid to take the initiative; telephone the personnel director or even the staff manager, if you know his or her name, to arrange a time for a personal interview.

Direct Mail Letter

A successful technique in a job campaign is to select a number of employers of your choice and simply send each a copy of your résumé with an individually written cover letter. Compile a list of prospective employers using professional journals, business directories, and other references. Learn as much as possible about the companies you have chosen. Address the letter to a specific person. Call the company and ask for the name of the personnel manager. Be sure to have the name spelled correctly.

Don't let this research overwhelm you; you're looking for a minimum of facts. If you are planning to send out fifty or more letters, research the ten or twelve companies in which you have the most interest. For the remaining organizations, it is enough to simply address the letter to the appropriate person and then mention the company name once or twice in the body of your letter. In essence, you are trying to make the letter appear as personal as possible, bearing in mind that most people don't read *form* letters.

In each letter point out the particular strengths and accomplishments that would be cf interest to the reader and indicate where they are described in your résumé. The tone of the letter should generate interest in you. Refer to a particular qualification that will demonstrate why it would be particularly advantageous to the potential employer to add you to its staff. Always discuss how you can be of value to them rather than how they can help you. Close with a courteous thank-you, and state that you will call in a few days to set up an appointment.

Letters to Employment Agencies

Start by calling each target employment agency and executive search firm in your area, and talking with—or get the name of—the highest ranking individual. In some cases, you might set up a meeting; in other instances, you'll get "permission" to send your résumé. For the out-of-town agencies or to those whose names are unavailable, simply address your covering letter to the president.

The purpose of your letter is to set up a conversation with the appropriate recruiter in each agency—best done in person; second best by phone. Request your résumé be kept on file so that you can be notified of any suitable job openings. Though we recommend that you discuss your feelings concerning relocation, the covering letter is not the place to mention salary requirements. You should keep your cover letter brief, but at the same time make reference to certain of your strengths.

On frequent occasions, executive recruiters rewrite résumés, (not always to the candidate's advantage), **you must ask them to show you your "rewritten" résumé before it is sent to a potential employer.** We cannot emphasize this too strongly!

The last paragraph, similar to the other types of cover letters, should include an indication that you will phone in a week or so to set up either a phone or a personal interview.

Letter to a Colleague or Friend

Colleagues, friends, or relatives can often be an excellent source of leads. For that reason, you should give them a copy of your résumé. When sending your résumé, include a short informal note instead of a businesslike covering letter. The note should simply say that you're in the process of seeking employment or attempting to change jobs and would appreciate any suggestions he or she can offer. You might mention how you feel about relocation. Mention if your job search is confidential. Don't discuss your salary requirements, but you might ask if it would be useful to send additional résumés.

Sample Cover Letters

16 4th Street
Ft. Lauderdale, Fla. 33311
(305) 162-4690

April 19, 1989

Mr. James Arter
Personnel Director
Sun & Tan, Inc.
1200 Biscayne Blvd.
Miami, Florida 33125

Dear Mr. Arter:

Please find the enclosed résumé in response to your advertisement for Sales, which appeared in the Miami Herald on Sunday, April 14, 1989.

Please note that I have had eight years' experience selling cosmetics and hair products for Jackson and Andrews. In this position I was responsible for the Florida, Alabama, and Georgia territory.

Realizing that this summary, as well as my résumé, cannot adequately communicate my qualifications in-depth, I would appreciate having the opportunity to discuss with you in person how I might become an asset to your company. I will call you early next week to set up an appointment for an interview. I look forward to meeting you.

Sincerely,

Amy Lawson

Amy Lawson

200 Erie Avenue
Rochester, N.Y. 14610
(716) 681-1144

May 12, 1989

Box 6214
Rochester Times
10 Broad Street
Rochester, N.Y. 14610

To Whom It May Concern:

I enclose my résumé in response to your sales advertisement in the
Rochester Times on Sunday, May 1.

My sales/marketing background includes an eight-year association with
Gordon's Sporting Goods, Inc., where I was in charge of developing the
New England territory. This involved recruiting, training, and working
with the sales force. It was also my responsibility to develop and
implement sales/marketing plans and strategies in support of the field
sales effort.

I am presently employed as Sales Manager of Woodrow and Martin, Inc., a
men's clothing manufacturer. I am very eager to return to the sporting
goods industry.

In my present position, I call on, sell, and service mass merchandisers,
retail chains, department stores, and military exchanges. I achieved
success in these and other related activities, and enjoy the fine rapport
and reputation developed through my ability to communicate and work with
people on all levels.

I am a results-oriented manager who enjoys traveling and working with
people, motivating them, and developing their skills to maximum potential.
It would be difficult to indicate every area of expertise in my résumé,
therefore I would appreciate meeting with you to discuss my qualifications
for this position in greater detail.

I will call to set up an appointment for an interview.

Sincerely,

Harry Ellis

Harry Ellis

29 Ridge Road
Elmira, New York 10623
April 14, 1989

Box X3349
New York Guardian
749 East 56th Street
New York, New York 10022

Dear Sir:

I am replying to your advertisement of this date offering a position as copy editor on a sports car publication.

As my résumé demonstrates, I have my B.S. in journalism
and have been working as copy writer and assistant copy
editor on magazines for the past six years.

Your ad specified an interest in and knowledge of
sports cars. I did not feel it appropriate to mention it
in my resume, but I am the owner of one of the few surviving
Type 57 Bugattis in this country, and have rebuilt and maintain the car myself. The car is registered with the Bugatti
Club of America to which I also belong. I hope this estab-
lishes my credentials as a sports car enthusiast.

If my background is of use to you, please contact me
at your convenience.

I appreciate your consideration.

Yours truly,

Anthony Lo Bello

Anthony Lo Bello

Encl.

16 Chilton Street
Cleveland, Ohio 40612
April 9, 1988

Mr. George Teasdale
Personnel Manager
United Chemical Corporation
452 Sorrent Drive
Teeterboro, New Jersey 11402

Dear Mr. Teasdale:

I am replying to your advertisement in the April issue of
Cosmetic Chemistry.

While having no specific background in cosmetic chemistry,
I would like to point out that my work with Basic Pharmaceutical's Anesthetic and Analgesic division consisted primarily of
developing and testing non-oleaginous bases for topical anes-
thetics. The basis, of course, had to be broadly anti-allergic
if they were to be of commercial value and were tested for same.
Our procedures, in both development and testing, were similar
to those used in the cosmetic industry, and our tests were at
least as rigorous.

My résumé also shows, as your ad requested, heavy Quantitative Analysis and Quality Control experience.

I would like to speak with you further. I will be in New
York for the Pharmaceutical Chemists' Society meeting next
month. Could we arrange an interview for that time?

Thank you for your consideration.

Yours truly,

John Villiers

John Villiers

Enclosure

320 Garrity Drive
Chicago, Illinois 11625
May 24, 1988

Mr. Henry Wilford
President
Seafarer's Museum
Xenobia, Maine 10874

Dear Mr. Wilford:

I am applying for a position with your museum as I feel my experience
in developing a Museum Sales Department will be of interest to you.

As my résumé indicates, I held the position as Sales Manager of Wood-
bury Reconstruction Company for six years. In this capacity, I
developed a mail order sales department and created a successful book-
shop specializing in native crafts.

I expect to be in the vicinity of Xenobia in the first week of July.
Could we arrange for an interview at that time? As I am currently
employed, I would appreciate this be kept in confidence.

Your consideration is greatly appreciated.

Sincerely yours,

Richard Shelton

Richard Shelton

Enclosure

14 Seegate Avenue
Grand Rapids, Michigan 49505

September 3, 1989

Mr. Ernest Chapman
Vice-President for Marketing
Cargon & Fuller, Inc.
280 Wall Street
Grand Rapids, Michigan 49505

Dear Mr. Chapman:

I believe my 10 years of solid marketing background would be an asset
to Cargon & Fuller, Inc.

In my association with General Dynamics, Inc., I was responsible for
increasing sales of a $40 million product line between 15% and 34% in
twenty markets after years of consistent decline. I also reversed
continual losses of a $150 million profit center and restored pro-
fitability to several smaller operations scheduled for write-offs.
I have also been successful in opening market areas previously
unknown to the company.

As you will see from the enclosed résumé I am also experienced in new
product development, acquisitions, licensing, and export. It is my
hope that Cargon & Fuller would be interested in a person with my
qualifications. I will be calling early next week to determine when
you will be able to set up an appointment to discuss a sales or
marketing position with your firm.

Sincerely,

Samuel Davis

Samuel Davis

2121 Toronto Street
Buffalo, N.Y. 14229
May 19, 1989

Mr. Arthur Bigelow
Personnel Director
Niagara Industries, Inc.
10 Chambers Street
Buffalo, N.Y. 14281

Dear Mr. Bigelow:

In September 1989, I will receive my Bachelor of Arts Degree in Marketing from the University of Buffalo, and I am interested in obtaining an entry-level position with your company. Friends have told me about Niagara, Inc., and I understand you have a superior marketing department.

My undergraduate studies covered a wide range with concentrations in statistics, economics, and law as well as in marketing. As such, I believe I have a strong business background and would work well in your organization.

I have enclosed my résumé showing my work experience during summers and part-time employment while in college. From this information, you will see that I am an active, motivated person and will continue this aggressiveness with your organization.

I look forward to meeting you in person and will call you next week to set up an appointment.

Sincerely,

Caroline Houston

Caroline Houston

26 James Street
Chicago, Illinois 60602
April 6, 1989

Mr. John Anderson
Personnel Director
Digital Corporation
Detroit, Michigan 51073

Dear Mr. Anderson:

I am a graduate student in Computer Science at Yale University, and I will be awarded an M.S. degree in June 1989. I am currently looking for a position related to Database/Graphics Package Design in the research and development department of a major company.

Before coming to Yale, I designed, supervised, and completed a CAD system. The function covers vector, character and curve generation, windowing, shading, and transformations.

At Yale, my research work involves Compilation of Relational Queries into Network DML. To enhance my background, I have taken some courses in Computer Graphics and Data Base, and I have experience in and understanding of the design of Database. With this strong background, I certainly believe that I am competent to meet challenging tasks and can make a good contribution to your company.

Enclosed please find my résumé, which indicates in some detail my training and experience. I sincerely hope that my qualifications are of interest to you and that an interview might be arranged at your convenience.

Thank you for your consideration and I am looking forward to hearing from you soon.

Sincerely yours,

Martha Levine

Martha Levine

Encl.

19 Bayside Lane
Bethesda, Md. 21058

July 21, 1989

Mr. Robert Nash
Vice-President of Sales
Nelson & Murphy Inc.
2100 Broad Street
Baltimore, MD. 21245

Dear Mr. Nash:

I am applying for a position as Sales Manager with your company, as I
feel my background in developing a sales department will be of interest
to you.

As my résumé indicates, I joined Kobin, Inc., in the capacity of a
trainee and moved up the ladder to my current position of Sales Manager.
In each year of my employment I was successful in opening new accounts,
penetrating existing ones, and reopening closed businesses. As a result,
I was responsible for sales increases of 20% to 25%.

As sales manager I was involved in recruiting, training, and supervising
a staff of 120 salespeople and was responsible for sales worldwide.

I am looking forward to meeting you in person and will call next week in
hopes of setting up an appointment for an interview.

Sincerely,

James Wilson

James Wilson

1900 Hillside Terrace
Boston, Mass. 02126
April 15, 1989

Mr. Donald Reed
Personnel Director
Chase & Morris, Inc.
615 Main Street
Boston, Mass. 02120

Dear Mr. Reed:

I am writing to you today in hope you will read my résumé and consider me for a marketing position with your company.

I was very interested in the article about your company which appeared in the New York Times on April 1, 1989. Your paternalistic policy which involves a "no-turn-over" company complies with both my short-term and long-range goals, as I am really interested in a stable opportunity.

As my résumé indicates, I offer 12 years of solid marketing experience. In my association with Stanley, Inc., my present employer, gross sales have increased by $15 million due to a concentrated Product Marketing Plan introduced by me.

I was also responsible for the development of strategies and implementation of a direct mail strategy for seven new packages and five offers, which resulted in a package that beat the control by 250%.

I will call early next week so that we can set up an interview in the hope that I can impress you as much as your company impresses me. Your consideration is greatly appreciated.

Sincerely yours,

Adam Stane

Adam Stane

Encl.

1800 Harrison Road
Los Angeles, CA 90063

April 30, 1989

Martha Livingston
Personnel Manager
Vogue Patterns, Inc.
100 Pace Street
Los Angeles, CA 90002

Dear Miss Livingston:

I believe my ten years of accounting experience might be an asset to Vogue Patterns and therefore I have enclosed my résumé for your consideration.

I was very impressed with the articles about your company, which appeared in the Los Angeles Times on Sunday, April 28, 1989. Your paternalistic policy, which involves a "no-turn-over" company, complies with both my short-term and long-range goals, as I am really interested in a stable opportunity.

In my ten-year association with Helen Curtis, I was fully responsible for the preparation of monthly consolidated financial statements for management and public reporting--Forms 10K, 10 2 and the Annual Report to Shareholders, and shared responsibility with the Corporate Controller in maintaining operating units compliance with the FASB and SEC pronouncements.

I will call you early next week so that we can set up an interview in the hope that I can impress you as much as your company impresses me. Your consideration is greatly appreciated.

Sincerely,

Anita Parsons

Anita Parsons

Encl.

18 Dogwood Lane
Hastings, NY 10706

June 16, 1989

Mrs. Dorothy Mitchell
Career Blazers Agency, Inc.
590 Fifth Ave.
New York, NY 10036

Dear Mrs. Mitchell:

Thank you for taking the time to discuss opportunities available to me through Career Blazers. As I mentioned in our conversation, I have nearly as much paralegal as legal secretarial experience. However, my interest at this time lies in the area of paralegal.

I am enclosing ten copies of my résumé as you suggested. You will notice that I have emphasized my paralegal expertise. I am particularly interested in a position in the metropolitan area and would consider a temporary assignment if it had potential to become permanent.

I expect to be in New York City in early July and will call to set up another meeting.

Sincerely,

Allen Oxman

Allen Oxman

Enclosure

106 East End Ave.
New York City, NY 10028
(212) 874-3614

January 16, 1989

Walker Associates
517 Fifth Ave.
New York City, NY 10017

Gentlemen:

I would appreciate it if you would place my enclosed
résumé in your files.

I graduated from Ohio State University in 1978 and my ten
years of financial experience consist of four years as controller
of a ladies ready-to-wear manufacturer, three years as assistant
controller in a sportswear firm, and three years as an accountant
with a book publisher.

My "hands-on" operations experience has included developing
professional accounting, reporting, and data processing
functions. My strengths include problem-solving, producing order
out of confusion, and getting things done.

I would like to discuss my salary requirements when we meet
at a personal interview. Because my time is flexible, I am
available to meet you at your convenience. I shall call early
next week to set up an appointment.

Sincerely,

Kenneth Newman

110 Tenth Ave.
New York City, NY 10011

May 10, 1989

Miss Anne Tully,
Personnel Director
Deeth & Johnson, Inc.
165 Madison Avenue
New York City, NY 10016

Dear Miss Tully:

In June, 1989, I will receive my Bachelor of Arts degree from
Columbia University and I am interested in obtaining an entry
level accounting position with your company.

As you will see from the enclosed résumé, I majored in
accounting, minored in economics, and maintained a 3.2 grade
average from my freshman through senior years. For the past three
summers I have been employed as a temporary accounting clerk by
Career Blazers Temporary Personnel, Inc. and my assignments have
included such agencies as Benton & Baroles, Cunningham & Walsh,
B.B.D. & Gray. These assignments convince me that my ultimate
career goal lies in the advertising industry.

Not noted in my résumé is my intention of returning to Columbia
University's evening sessions to pursue an MBA in accounting and
business.

I will call early next week in hopes of setting up an appointment
for an interview. I feel confident that I can convince you that
I have the qualifications to become an asset to Deeth & Johnson.

Sincerely,

Karen Reed

Karen Reed

14 Sommers St.
Newburgh, NY 12550
May 10, 1989

Miss Lynn Brown
Career Blazers Agency, Inc.
590 Fifth Ave.
New York, NY 10036

Dear Miss Brown:

I've been told by several personnel directors in the publishing field that Career Blazers specializes in placing recent college graduates. I will receive my Bachelor of Arts degree in English from Skidmore College in September, 1989, and am interested in obtaining an editorial position with a book or magazine publisher.

As my résumé indicates, I maintained a 3.5 average for my four years in college and worked as a Friday for the Skidmore Office of University Systems for three years (1985-1988), part-time during school and full-time through the summers and other vacations. I am an excellent typist, and though I am not looking for a secretarial position, I would be willing to exchange my typing skill and secretarial expertise for an entry level position with potential.

I am looking forward to meeting you in the near future and will call you early next month to set up an interview.

Yours truly,

Nancy Hanks
Nancy Hanks

1900 Driftwood Drive
No. Miami Beach, Florida 33160
August 25, 1989

Ms. Nola Chestor
Management Recruiters, Inc.
180 Collins Avenue
Miami, Florida 33139

Dear Ms. Chestor:

I am enclosing a copy of my résumé in hopes that your firm
may assist me in locating a position as Corporate Controller with
a Fortune 500 company.

As my résumé indicates, I have ten years experience in
Financial Management and Control, having served in the past as
Treasurer, Controller, Corporate Accountant, Consolidation
Manager and Director of Financial Planning. In my present
position at Thompson Chemical Corp., I initiate, develop, and
supervise all internal audits.

As I have not yet given notice, I would appreciate your
discretion in this matter.

I am looking forward to meeting you in person at which time
I can explain in depth both my qualifications and aspirations. I
will call early next week to set up a personal meeting.

Yours truly,

Warren Barth

Carl Ferguson
16 South Street
Darien, Connecticut 06490
February 8, 1989

Ms. Patricia Schwartz
Taft Computer Company
1800 Broad Street
Philadelphia, Pennsylvania 20171

Dear Patricia:

It was a very pleasant surprise running into you at the Philadelphia
Computer Show this morning. I have enclosed my resume, so that it may be
circulated to the appropriate department heads, when you contact them.

As we discussed today, I am interested in working for Taft in the
Philadelphia area and in dealing with customers. An experienced software
specialist, I have proposed, planned, designed, managed, developed, and
delivered major software systems to users. Project management of a multi-
person effort has been the primary responsibility of my latest job. In
addition to having management and technical skills, I enjoy people, giving
presentations, and consulting. Taft appears to offer opportunities in
marketing, customer support, and development that would use my computing
expertise, along with my verbal abilities.

Having recently delivered a significant software application, I would
like to begin a new challenge as soon as possible.

I am looking forward to hearing from you soon, and establishing the
next step in our discussion. I will call next week to set up our next
meeting.

Talking with you was a pleasure and has given me a very positive impression
of Taft as a company.

Yours truly,

Carl Ferguson

encl.

474 Hardscrabble Road
Millville, New York 10901
April 4, 1989

Ms. Bernice Luddington
Art Director
Abington's Department Store
1502 Mamaroneck Avenue
White Plains, New York   10603

Dear Ms. Luddington:

 The controller of your Paramus branch, William Scott, who is a neighbor
of mine, has told me that you have an opening for a display designer in
your White Plains Store.

 As you can see from my résumé, I had extensive experience in the field
prior to the birth of my first child. While I have been unable to seek
employment in the field for several years, I have kept my hand in, as
it were, by designing displays of art and handicrafts as a volunteer at
our local library.

 My youngest child is now in high school and able to take care of himself. In addition, my sister lives nearby and has agreed to take care
of any emergency that might arise; so, I will be able to devote myself
wholeheartedly to my job.

 I would welcome an opportunity to speak with you. Could I call your
secretary for an appointment?

 Thank you for your consideration.

                                        Yours sincerely,

                                        Helen Fries

Enclosure

95 Valentine Lane
Melville, NY 11747
June 8, 1989

Ms. Jane Raymond
Personnel Director
North Bank of America
White Plains, NY 10603

Dear Ms. Raymond:

   Mr. John Smith, an executive in your Manhattan office, who is a friend of my father, suggested I write to you about the possibililty of an opening in your international department.

   As you can see from my résumé, I am a French major and Spanish minor and am very interested in a position where I can use my knowledge of languages. I have worked as an office temporary for the past three summers and some of my assignments were in the banking field. I am a good typist (70 wpm) and would be quite willing to start in a clerical capacity.

   I would like very much to meet you and am available for an interview any time convenient to you.

Sincerely yours,

John Osterio

3200 Bayview Drive
Scarsdale, NY 10583
April 11, 1989

Ms. Claire Lunt
Beacon Press, Inc.
16 W. 49th St.
New York City, NY 10020

Dear Ms. Lunt:

Rita Marks, an editorial assistant with your company, told me of your plans to expand your accounting department. For that reason, plus my avocational interest in books, I am enclosing a copy of my résumé in hopes that my background will be of interest to you.

I am a graduate of Columbia University (June 1987) with a degree in accounting and economics, which emphasized taxation and managerial accounting. I will receive a Master of Business Administration from Columbia University in June 1989. For the past three summers I worked as an accounting clerk with Shiller & Rogers and, because some of their clients are involved in publishing, I have gained some actual experience in accounting for the book industry.

I feel sure that I have the education, experience, potential, and enthusiasm to be successful with your firm and would appreciate an opportunity for a personal interview. I will call you in a few days to set up an appointment.

Thanking you in advance for any courtesies, I remain

Sincerely,

Lillian Robbins

Lillian Robbins

119 Grattan Ave.
Oyster Bay, NY 11771
Dec. 19, 1988

Roger Smaridge, Controller
General Rent-A-Car, Inc.
118 W. Second Avenue
Dayton, OH 45424

Dear Mr. Smaridge:

Nadine Foster, an attorney with your company and a long time friend, recently told me about an opening for a tax accountant at General Rent-A-Car, Inc. I feel that I am extremely qualified for that position and I have enclosed a résumé for your consideration.

As you can see from my résumé, I have over ten years experience in the area of tax accountancy. In my present position with the Whitney Bowes Credit Corporation, I am heavily involved in property and sales tax research, which includes finding solutions to problems unique to the leasing industry. I am also responsible for any property tax appeals and audits that might affect Whitney Bowes. I have also gained expertise in the preparation of income and franchise tax in selected states.

I would appreciate an opportunity for a personal meeting, at whch time I hope I can convince you that I can be a very important asset to General Rent-A-Car.

I will call you next week to set up an interview.

Yours truly,

Patrick Johnson

41 Cumberland Drive
Scarsdale, New York
10583

Sept. 18, 1989

Mr. Bob Brody, President
Walker Brody Personnel, Inc.
509 Fifth Avenue
New York, New York 10017

Dear Mr. Brody:

Bill Lewis of Career Blazers Personnel Services, Inc. suggested you might
be of assistance to me in my desire to find new employment. I became
acquainted with Bill while I was Assistant Controller at Parker Press.

As you can see from my enclosed résumé, all of my accounting experience
has been in publishing. I started with R. R. Majors, Inc., then Parker Press,
and am presently employed as Controller in Walker & Walker & Co. As
you've probably heard, Walker & Walker is moving to Washington, DC and
because it is now imperative that I remain in the metropolitan area, I am
available for a new position. Bill spoke very highly of you and I am looking
forward to getting together with you to discuss my background and qualifications in depth.

I'll call you at the end of next week in hopes of arranging a date that will be
mutually convenient.

Yours truly,

Bob Miller

Bob Miller

1440 N.W. 56th Ave.
Tampa, FL 33610

July 17, 1989

Dear Mike,

I'm finally taking your advice and decided to pull up stakes and make the move to New York City.

Just last week I gave notice at Peat & Marvich and I think we actually found a buyer for our condo down here. We plan to move in with Jan's mother and then slowly look for either a co-op in the city or ultimately buy a house in Westchester County.

As you probably remember, all of my experience has been in public accounting, but I would consider any opportunity that offers both stability and potential.

I'd really appreciate any suggestions you might have that could be helpful in finding a job. If you know any employment agencies or executive recruiters that specialize in financial personnel, please let me know of them.

I'm enclosing a few copies of my résumé. Because I've already given notice, please feel free to circulate them.

We should be in New York in mid-September and will call as soon as we get settled. Jan and I are looking forward to seeing you and Louise again.

Yours truly,

Bill

Bill

19 Seneca Lake Avenue
Elmira, N.Y. 14901

November 19, 1989

Ms. Phyllis Grey
General Elevator, Inc.
1200 Meadow Drive
Elmira, N.Y. 14901

Dear Ms. Grey,

John Evans, a programmer with your company, suggested I send
my résumé to you. John and I met while we attended Hobart
College.

As my résumé indicates, I have solid background in sales and
though I haven't had industrial experience, I minored in
electrical engineering and feel I have an aptitude in any
technical area. I understand you are expanding your sales
staff and would greatly appreciate your consideration.

I am looking forward to meeting you in the near future and
will call you early next week.

Yours truly,

George Clancy

George Clancy

140 Wenkover Road
Cleveland, Ohio   44112
March 30, 1989

Dear Yvette,

I ran into Dick Smith last week and he suggested I get in touch with you. Gene has been transferred to Dallas, so I decided to leave Pacific Records and try to get a job in that area.

Since I last saw you, I've been promoted to a marketing position but will consider any opportunity in either marketing or sales. I would prefer a job without a lot of travel but will consider any opportunity as long as it is based in the Dallas area.

I'd really appreciate any suggestions you might have that could be helpful in finding a job. If you know of any employment agencies that place sales and marketing people, please let me know about them.

I'm enclosing 6 copies of my résumé. Since I've already given notice, feel free to circulate them as you see fit.

We should be in Dallas by July. I'm looking forward to seeing you and Jim, and once again being neighbors.

Sincerely,

Margo

1400 State Street
Albany, New York 18246

May 15, 1989

Dear Ruth,

As you probably know, Paris Records has been sold to National Records and I've been merged out of a job. Though there are a few possibilities in this area, I think this might be the perfect time for me to relocate to Florida. It would be great to be near my old friends and, as you know, I've always loved the warm weather.

I'm hoping that one of your firms' clients has an opening that fits my qualifications. I'm enclosing several copies of my résumé for you to circulate at your discretion. Should you need more résumés, please let me know.

I'd really appreciate any suggestions you might have that could be helpful in my finding a job. Can you recommend any search firms/agencies that service the financial field?

I plan to be in Ft. Lauderdale in early July, but could fly down earlier if necessary.

I'm really looking forward to seeing you soon and am grateful for anything you might do.

Love,

Marge

Where Do You Find Work?

6

Look Around You

A job search, like charity, begins at home. Of all the various job sources, the most convenient—and at times, the best—are your relatives, friends, and neighbors. Almost anyone you know may be able to furnish you with the lead you've been looking for. So, if you're on the job market, don't keep it quiet; part of your campaign is to let as many people as possible know that you are job hunting.

Don't be embarrassed about spreading the word. Your friends, too, have been in your position and know that any help is welcome. Were the positions reversed and a friend asked you for help, wouldn't you be eager to assist in any way you could?

Often people who are employed hear of job openings in their companies before the jobs are advertised or listed with employment agencies. Not only are they the first to know about the vacancies, but companies do tend to give preference in hiring to people recommended by their own employees rather than to a complete stranger. Often, at my agency, when following up one of our applicants, we have found out that the job went to a friend of an employee even though we knew our applicant was a perfect "fit" with both the job and the company.

Even though a "friend at court" is no guarantee of getting a job, it is far more likely that you will reach the interview stage if recommended by an employee of that company than would someone answering an ad or sent by an agency. In job hunting you always have to contend with human nature. An employer feels more secure about a prospect referred by someone he knows than about a complete stranger. Wouldn't you?

Now—if you are convinced of the foregoing and believe that someone you know is going to be instrumental in finding you a job, you are going to wonder if you shouldn't put off preparing a résumé until it's "needed." We agree. You shouldn't go to the trouble and expense of preparing a résumé until it *is* needed, and it is needed the moment you decide to look for work. If a friend or relative suggests your name to his company, it is almost certain that he or she will get back to you and say, "I've told them about you and they're interested, but first they want to see a résumé."

It is often a good idea to give the people you know copies of your résumé. It helps them in talking about you to people they think can help you, and in addition, they can speed up the decision process by handing in the résumé for you.

Networking is a new word for a process that job seekers have used since we evolved from feudal times and individuals sought employment. It is essentially a method of creating an ever expanding network of people who can help each other accomplish a specific goal, whether it be making a sale, finding an apartment, building a roster of clients or finding the right job.

Go about your networking in a professional, organized fashion. Start out by making a list of anybody who might supply you with leads: acquaintances of your spouse; people you know from school, adult education courses, avocational activities, P.T.A., clubs, volunteer and religious groups; and even your doctor, lawyer, or stockbroker. Expand your network by including fraternity brothers or sorority sisters, coworkers, and members of your alumni association.

In addition, put yourself in situations where you are likely to meet people who can help you—political organizations, community groups, class reunions, and professional associations.

(To get information about organizations in your field, ask your librarian for such reference books as *Gayles' Encyclopedia of Associations* and the *National Trade and Professional Associations*, Columbia Books, Inc., Washington, D.C.)

Classified Ads

Read the ads! There is a wealth of information in the classified columns of your newspaper. You may not find the job of your dreams (although you might), but you can learn much about the job market by going over the classified ads. You will see what kinds of jobs are open and can get an idea about salaries in the various fields. Through the ads, you have a means of testing whether the salary you're hoping for is in line with reality, or, for that matter, whether your job expectations are realistic.

When searching the ads, consider all job titles. An opening for a bookkeeper, for example, may be listed under "Accounting"; an administrative assistant's position could be advertised as "Executive Secretary." Don't let the job titles mislead you; read the entire body of the ad. The duties required and the qualifications desired give much more information about the job than can its title. The vocabulary of job hunting can overwhelm you with its confusion. An assistant to an editor might be advertised as "Editorial Assistant," "Secretary to the Editor," "Guy/Gal Friday," or even "Publishing Assistant."

Be careful not to ignore a good opportunity simply because the job title is not what you might have expected. Be sure to read the classified section carefully and respond to every ad that might be a "possible." Remember, too, that salaries are approximate. Very often jobs are filled at salaries higher or lower than those offered in the ads. Ultimately, salary depends upon the qualifications of the person selected. For this reason, it is advisable to answer all ads (with which your qualifications coincide to some degree) even if the salary offered is in the extreme lower limit of your range. A job listed at $15,000 might be filled eventually at a salary of $18,000 or one advertised as "to $13,000" might go only to $11,000. In addition, a job listed at a salary less than you had anticipated could offer so much growth and opportunity that it might bear investigation.

Because you are looking for the best possible job, it is advisable to explore as many opportunities as possible, to present yourself at as many interviews as you can, and to learn as much about each job offered as you are able. Then, after careful consideration of each job with all of its opportunities, benefits, and ramifications, you accept the one that most closely resembles what you are looking for.

Be sure to follow the directions given in each particular ad. If a phone number is listed and it is requested that you call for an appointment, do so; don't arrive without warning. Some job seekers think that an unannounced arrival shows great enthusiasm. It doesn't. What it does is waste both your and the interviewer's time, and creates hostility. If a box number is listed, reply by sending your résumé with a covering letter as discussed in Chapter 5.

Don't be discouraged if you don't get immediate results. At times, as much as three months can elapse before your receiving a response to your résumé. Remember that job hunting is harder and more frustrating than working, but once you have had success in your search, the weeks, or even months of anxiety and anguish will be forgotten very quickly.

Private Employment Agencies

Anyone out job hunting should consider the services of the private employment agency. Their business consists of trying to find the right people for the jobs and the right jobs for the people. They might be able to offer you the help you need. The private agencies recruit and screen applicants for many different firms and, therefore, are in a position to introduce you to a number of prospective employers.

Therefore, going to an employment agency is equivalent to applying for a variety of job openings. The agency can describe every opening that it has listed that could be filled by a person with your qualifications and leave you the choice of which ones you want to investigate further. Effectively, the agency does your legwork for you and will keep you informed of new job openings as they arise. Most agencies expect and need résumés, and you should be prepared to give them several copies.

Private agencies charge a fee, which may be paid by the job seeker or the employer or be divided between them. The fee is charged only in the event that the agency finds you a job that you are willing to accept. Be sure that you fully understand what the remuneration agreement is. If you are asked to sign a contract, ascertain precisely what you are committed to before you accept a job. Today it is more customary for the employer to pay the full fee, but many agencies still have jobs listed where the applicant must pay. Some employers may prefer to reimburse the employee for the fee after a certain length of employment. Don't feel embarassed to ask the interviewer at the agency to clarify any questions about the contract. As with any other business arrangement, it is best to have a complete understanding of terms at the very beginning of your relationship with the agency.

Finding the appropriate agency is also a very important consideration on the job hunt. Most agencies specialize in certain fields or professions; so, be sure that the agencies you register with handle your skills or professional qualifications. If you are a graduate engineer, there is no point in registering with an agency that specializes in accountants and bookkeepers. Study the agencies' ads in the classified columns of the newspaper; the types of jobs they advertise will generally indicate their area of specialization.

Because employment agencies are completely involved in recruiting, they can be helpful in advice about current job trends and market conditions. Quite often, too, they are able to assume some of the functions of the trained guidance counselor. Because they are in continual touch with the job market, they are able to see that your particular skills may be appropriate to an industry that you had never considered worth investigating.

A few years ago, my agency interviewed a young man who was what is often called "over qualified." He had a Ph.D. in Romance Languages, was completely bilingual in Spanish and English, and had reading and writing ability in French and Italian. He did not want to teach and had followed up what he considered to be every lead for a person of his training—United Nations, foreign embassies and consulates, import-export firms, multinational corporations, and so on. The offers he received, he had refused, because he felt the salaries were completely unrealistic. We agreed with him, but didn't feel we could do anything at the moment for him. His résumé was passed around the office and our law desk called one of her accounts that had a heavy international practice. Unfortuantely the applicant needed a law degree to go with the bilingualism. Three days later, however, the law firm called back suggesting we contact an underwriter at a large marine insurance company. The outcome was that the applicant found a job at the managerial level and commensurate pay in a field that he had never considered.

For an agency to find a job in this manner—where an employer account unable to take an applicant suggests that the agency try to place him with another particular company—is not unusual. You have to consider your counselor at the agency as your ally. The agency wants to place you and it wants to place you in the best job available for you. That is its function and, if it wants to stay in business, it has to perform it.

State and Government Employment Agencies

Another fine source of job leads is the state or government employment agency. Unlike private, commercial agencies, government agencies charge no fee to either the job applicant or the employer. Their functions are supported by the government.

If you are serious about your job search, you should visit your local government employment office to avail yourself of its services. In addition to advising you of job openings in the immediate vicinity, the counselors at these agencies can also give you information on obtaining a government job.

Government Jobs

Don't overlook the possibilities that government can offer. The U.S. government employs over 17 million Americans. One out of 6 employed persons serve either federal, state, or local governments. The federal government employs 2.8 million, the state government employs 4 million, and local government over 8 million. U.S. government agencies hire 13,000-18,000 recent college grads a year. These statistics represent a significant portion of the work force and, therefore, a government position is an option that should be taken seriously.

The range of job offerings is tremendous. Doctors, attorneys, secretaries, clerks are employed by the government, as well as teachers, engineers, gardeners, and chauffeurs. Think of a job classification and rest assured that the government employs people in that category. Many people feel that the government jobs offer the most security (or *did* until the last recession), the best health plans, the most liberal vacations, and the most extensive retirement plans.

The government, perhaps, is the only employer that is not interested in your résumé. Governmental positions have precise and inflexible educational and experiental requirements that must be met in order to *apply* for a given job. All that meeting these requirements entitles you to is the opportunity to take an examination for the job. The examination is both determinative and competitive. That is, you must achieve a certain grade in order to be eligible for the job, but the job will be offered first to the person who achieved the highest score on the test. Depending upon the job, the test may be written, practical, or physical. A sanitation engineer must be strong enough to lift a garbage pail, and a chauffeur must be able to drive, not merely know the traffic rules and the simple repair of a car.

Should you take a test for a government job and not score high enough to fill one of the immediately available openings, you may be eligible for subsequent openings. Usually, each "class" taking the examination retains its eligibility for a certain period of time, and during that time no additional examinations are given. Customarily, examinations are given every six months, every year, or every two or three years. As a rule, if you are still interested in a position when an examination occurs again, you must take the exam again to determine your eligibility.

Should you be interested in government employment, you have to be very methodical in seeking it out. You must find out what the offerings are that might be available immediately and in the future at every government level. There is no single office that takes care of federal, state, county, and municipal employment; each has to be applied for in its appropriate office.

On the municipal level, a call to your city or town hall will tell you where to go and whom to see. For county employment, another phone call will start the ball rolling. On the search for employment with your state government, you should check the phone book to see if there is an office of the State Civil Service Commission (or Personnel Board) near you. If not, you should write to the State Civil Service Commission requesting a list of current examinations and job openings.* You should also ask to be put on their regular mailing list. In this manner you will obtain continuous up-to-date information.

The main post office in your town will have some information on examinations and openings in the Federal Civil Service.** More complete information may be obtained from the nearest local office of the Federal Civil Service Commission or from the main office in Washington, D.C. Again, you should request to be put on the regular mailing list. It is worth noting that U.S. government jobs are available abroad as well as within the United States.

If you are interested in government work, stay with it. Read all of the literature available—your local library is a fine source. Take all tests for which you are eligible. There are enormous

---

* See also *Barron's How to Prepare for Civil Service Examinations* (Clerks, Typists, Stenographers, and Other Office Positions).
** See also *Barron's How to Prepare for the Professional and Administrative Career Examination (PACE)*. This exam may be taken by those holding the bachelor's degree or having the equivalent in working and/or education/working experience.

opportunities in government, and it is likely that your perseverance will get you the job you want.

Chamber of Commerce

Your Chamber of Commerce can be extremely helpful in your
job search. It can supply you with a list of all of the companies
in your area. Such a list would be excellent for your personal
direct mail campaign. You might even learn from the Chamber
of Commerce of actual job openings and which companies
would be most interested in your skills and qualifications.

Temporary Services

Temporary services can be extremely useful. Not only are they
a means of supporting yourself during your job campaign, but
they can even help you in getting the kind of job you really want.
They are especially of value to beginners, people in the intermediate level, and those returning to the job market after an
absence.

Most job seekers tend to overlook this source. They feel that,
as their goal is a *permanent* position, they have nothing to gain
by taking temporary employment. On the surface this would
appear logical, but it does not consider the fact that a temporary
position is often the opening wedge of the perfect job opportunity. Quite often, my agency has found that while our permanent division is recruiting for a specific job, our temporary
division has sent a "temp" to cover the position until it was filled.
We have become accustomed to learning that the "temp" was
hired on a permanent basis.

It makes sense. Whereas temps are often hired to provide
extra force during an occasional moment of surge in a
company's work load or to fill in for a sick or vacationing
employee, they are also called in to keep the work from piling up
on a desk that has unexpectedly become vacant. Although the
original intention is to interview other people to fill the job, the
temp is on the spot demonstrating a capability for the job. No
longer an unknown applicant, the temp often will be hired
ahead of a person replying to an ad offering the permanent
position. Often, too, the temp being a proven worker, the salary
offer will be higher than that listed in the "specs" for the
permanent position.

We had interviewed a highly experienced copywriter who had
lost his job because of a slow advertising market. As our
permanent division had nothing to offer him at the time, he
asked if our temporary division could find him something—

anything. As he explained, he was basically a lazy person and felt that any length of time collecting unemployment insurance would be psychologically disastrous for him. He also preferred to work as an office temporary rather than be overqualified in a permanent position.

Our temporary division sent him to a major oil company as a typist. As the gesture wouldn't cost him anything, he took his résumé along and left it with personnel. After working a few weeks as a typist, he was hired for an editorial position on the company's house organ. This position was not even known to us, as the oil company hadn't even gotten around to listing it!

A young woman came to us a few years ago with aspirations of getting into the publishing field. She had no previous experience, having just graduated from college, and in addition, she was job hunting at a time when most publishing houses were cutting back on staff. Desperate for work, she took temporary assignments, going from one company to another working as a clerk/typist. While filling in at the offices of a professional engineering society, she was offered a job as editorial assistant in their publications department. She called us a short time ago asking us to recruit an editorial assistant for her; she had been promoted to a full editorial position. The most remarkable part of this incident is that if we had received a call for an editorial assistant from the engineering society, we never would have sent that woman. In our previous dealings with them, they had always insisted on some engineering background for employees in their publications department. This woman, however, being on the spot, was able to demonstrate that her other skills and her intelligence more than made up for the deficiency in her background.

In the job search it is always advisable to take any opportunity that lets you get your foot in the door and prove your capabilities. In addition to offering this, it also permits you to enlarge your list of contacts by meeting new people. It is not unusual for your supervisor on a temporary job, impressed by your work and learning that you are marking time until you can find a permanent position, to suggest possibilities and leads you wouldn't have found otherwise.

It is important, therefore, while working as a temp, to do the best job you can and let everyone you meet know that you're looking for a permanent position. You never know who will introduce you to your new employers; so, bring copies of your résumé with you and leave one or two with anyone who shows interest in helping you.

Another advantage of the temporary services is that they can be extremely helpful to beginners or to persons who are not yet sure where their interests lie. Temporary work lets you experiment, spending a few days in one industry, perhaps a week or so in an art gallery, or possibly a month with a nonprofit organization. It is a way of seeing how each field works and helping you collect information necessary for a wise and considered career choice.

Working on temporary assignments brings no guarantee of a permanent job offer, but there is a guarantee that you'll meet a variety of people, be exposed to many different kinds of businesses, and experience various distinctive working conditions. Most important of all, you will be gaining additional experience—all of this while getting paid for it! By all means, give serious consideration to do temporary work while on your quest for a permanent job.

Volunteer Work

It may seem strange, but occasionally it can be profitable for you to work for nothing. Volunteer work, like temporary work, is a way of meeting people. As we cannot stress enough, the more people you meet, the greater the possibility that someone will be able to point you in the direction of your dream job. Another consideration to bear in mind is that volunteer work can give you the opportunity of improving skills that are not yet sufficiently developed for remunerative employment.

One of the unexpected delights about volunteer work is that you never know with whom you might be working. Some of those people you see answering the phones on educational television stations during fund-raising campaigns are very high-salaried executives of established companies. One of New York's leading industrial designers spends his Saturdays with three other volunteers at the sales desk of a New York museum. The wife of the owner of one of New York's finest French restaurants spends her Wednesday evenings in the company of ten to twelve other people—most of whom couldn't afford a meal in her husband's establishment—stuffing envelopes for a nonprofit organization.

Not only can you meet people who might help you find a job, but at times the volunteer work itself can become a paid position.

The woman who directs the display department of a large upstate New York museum first started with them ten years ago when it was only a *small* upstate New York museum. Growing nonprofit organizations often recruit new employees from the ranks of their volunteers.

Even if your volunteer work does not lead, directly or indirectly, to a job, it is a way of filling empty time and can also fill other voids in your life. You meet people who share interests similar to your own, as well as people who range across a far wider social and economic scale than you would normally meet. Even if you ignore the fact that you are doing a "good deed," it is not time wasted.

You cannot claim to have done all that is possible to find work if you have not conducted a direct mail campaign. Obviously, your résumé will be an integral part of this campaign; so, once you have prepared the best possible résumé, you are ready to start.

With your résumé ready, your next task is to compile a list of possible employers. If you want to work where you live or within commuting distance of your home town, the Yellow Pages of your telephone directory is one of your best possible sources. If you are willing to relocate, the reference librarian at your local library will be an excellent source of information for you. She can refer you to the books you need to compile your list. As a rule, you are not allowed to withdraw these books, but will have to prepare your list in the library's reference room. Because you will probably find you need other information as you go along, this is not a great inconvenience.

The list should not be too long. You don't want to feel that you have involved yourself in an interminable project. Bear in mind that every company on the list is going to be sent a covering letter with your résumé. This requires that you determine the names and title of the person to whom you plan to write. Such reference books as Standard and Poor's can give you this information. Again, the reference librarian can help you.

If you are willing to relocate, do not hesitate to write to companies at a distance from your home. Most companies, when faced by a really "hot" applicant, will either send someone to interview the applicant or pay for the applicant's trip to their main offices. If you are willing to relocate, you should so state on your résumé; otherwise, the company is apt to assume that you are looking for an opening in their office near your home.

Your cover letter should be brief and written in a conversational, but not "cute," tone. Simply say that you are enclosing your résumé and would like to be considered for a position in that company. Also include a short statement indicating why you feel your qualifications will interest the firm. As you are enclosing a résumé, which gives a detailed description of your talents and skills, there is no need to be too verbose in your covering letter.

The letter should never exceed four paragraphs. Your final paragraph should state that you will call in a few days hoping to arrange for an interview. *Don't wait for them to call.* The closer you come to personal contact, the closer you are to a job offer.

I cannot overemphasize the need to type *individually* every cover letter. You may reproduce your résumé; never your letter. The letter should have the format of a standard business letter with sufficient margin all around to present an attractive appearance. Don't forget that it is your first introduction to a prospective employer.

Following Through

7

Keeping a Record

Keep a record of each résumé sent and note the dates of your calls and interviews. Also indicate the results of each call and interview, and remember your follow-up letters. Don't leave anything to your memory; maintain a written record.

The simplest way of maintaining a record of your direct mail campaign is to make a carbon copy of each cover letter as you type it. On the bottom of the carbon, you can note date and result of your phone call, date of interview, result of interview, and follow-up note. These can be kept in a file folder with a separate sheet—or calendar page—with dates and times of interviews noted. It would be disastrous to set up two interviews for the same time.

A second system is to set up a large sheet of paper with column headings across the top of the sheet. The information, of course, would be the same as that maintained by using carbon copies. Below is the suggested heading for each column. The headings would be separated by lines drawn vertically down the full length of the sheet, and horizontal lines would be drawn, each about two inches below the other, to separate the entries for each company written. I suggest the following headings:

Résumé Mailing	Follow-Up Phone Call	Interview	Thank-You Letter	Job Offer	Confirmation or *"No Thank You, But"* Letter
Name	Date	Date	Date	Yes	Date
Title	Results	Time		No	Letter Type
Company		Interviewer			
Address		Results			
Date Sent					

> Note that record-keeping sheets of this type have been provided on pages 80 through 83 for your convenience.

The third system involves the use of 4" × 6" index cards. Again the information would be the same as the other systems. Below is a sample layout for the card:

Mr. Richard Rowe   Mailed 3/22/88
Chief Draftsman
Systems, Inc.
424 Park Place
Buford, PA 21370

Phone Call:_____
                                    (indicate date)

(Note results) _____

Interview:_____
                        (indicate date, time, and interviewer)

(Note results) _____

Thank-You Letter_____
                                    (indicate date)

Job Offer_____

Confirmation *or* "No Thank You, But" Letter_____
                                                (indicate date and letter type)

This system is the best for a very large mailing. I suggest that you have the index cards printed up cheaply rather than trying to type them yourself.

A direct mail campaign is not an inexpensive way of looking for work, but no way really is. Direct mail involves an expenditure of money—for reproduction of résumés, envelopes, postage, and phone calls—and time. But any other method involves as much time. The difference is that the direct mail time is spent in the comfort of your home instead of on buses, on the pavement, and in waiting rooms. If you are pounding the pavements looking for work, you also have expenses for car fare, lunches, and the continual cups of coffee. I point this out mainly to remind you that the job hunt is going to cost you regardless of how you do it. You've got to spend in order to earn.

Sample Follow-Up Notes

May 7, 1988

Mr. Richard Trump
Director of Social Work
Rockland Hospital
Rockland, Connecticut   06013

Dear Mr. Trump:

I regret that your job offer came a day too late. Just yesterday, I accepted a job as a social worker for another hospital. I am really sorry because I was impressed with your institution and probably would have fit in very well.

As I am not at all sure how my new job is going to work out, would you please be kind enough to keep my application on file, and contact me if there is another opening in the next few months?

Thank you for your offer, and again, I am sorry I have to refuse it.

Sincerely,

Anne Paulson

Anne Paulson

79 Coastal Highway
Miami Beach, Florida 33110
September 7, 1989

Mr. Marc Thomas
Leisure Realty Corporation
Miami, Florida 33133

Dear Mr. Thomas,

I just wanted to write to tell you how pleased I was to meet
with you last Wednesday.

I was particularly impressed with the quality of homes you
are constructing in Glen Garry and Boca Raton, and the
total-market concept your organization has used to shape
these developments.

Thank you for considering me for the position of Sales Agent
at Leisure Realty.

I look forward to hearing from you.

Sincerely,

John Villiers

John Villiers

September 22, 1988

Ms. Joanna Crosley
Marketing Director
The Johnson Crumpf Company
1435 Commonwealth Avenue
Boston, Massachusetts 02117

Dear Ms. Crosley:

I am delighted to confirm my acceptance of the job
as Senior Marketing Analyst. As you already know, I
am not going to report for another two weeks. But I
have just given my present firm two weeks' notice, and
will report to you on October 4th.

Let me reiterate how pleased I am at getting this
job. I was hoping that I would, as I feel that it is
the perfect job for me and I know that I will fit into
your company well.

Until October 4th, I am

Sincerely,

Barton Rockwood

Barton Rockwood

Résumé Mailing

Name _____

Title _____

Company _____

Address _____

Date Sent _____

Follow-Up Phone Call

Date _____

Results _____

_____

_____

_____

Interview

Date _____

Time _____

Interviewer _____

Results _____

Thank-You Letter

Date _____

_____

Job Offer

Yes _____

No _____

Confirmation or "No Thank You, But" Letter

Date _____

Letter Type _____

_____

Résumé Mailing

Name _____

Title _____

Company _____

Address _____

Date Sent _____

Follow-Up Phone Call

Date _____

Results _____

_____

_____

_____

Interview

Date _____

Time _____

Interviewer _____

Results _____

Thank-You Letter

Date _____

_____

Job Offer

Yes _____

No _____

Confirmation or "No Thank You, But" Letter

Date _____

Letter Type _____

_____

Résumé Mailing

Name _____

Title _____

Company _____

Address _____

Date Sent _____

Follow-Up Phone Call

Date _____

Results _____
_____
_____

Interview

Date _____

Time _____

Interviewer _____

Results _____
_____

Thank-You Letter

Date _____
_____

Job Offer

Yes _____

No _____

Confirmation or "No Thank You, But" Letter

Date _____

Letter Type _____
_____

Résumé Mailing

Name _____

Title _____

Company _____

Address _____

Date Sent _____

Follow-Up Phone Call

Date _____

Results _____
_____
_____

Interview

Date _____

Time _____

Interviewer _____

Results _____
_____

Thank-You Letter

Date _____
_____

Job Offer

Yes _____

No _____

Confirmation or "No Thank You, But" Letter

Date _____

Letter Type _____
_____

Résumé Mailing

Name _____

Title _____

Company _____

Address _____
_____

Date Sent _____

Follow-Up Phone Call

Date _____

Results _____
_____
_____

Interview

Date _____

Time _____

Interviewer _____
_____

Results _____

Thank-You Letter

Date _____
_____

Job Offer

Yes _____

No _____

Confirmation or "No Thank You, But" Letter

Date _____

Letter Type _____
_____

Résumé Mailing

Name _____

Title _____

Company _____

Address _____
_____

Date Sent _____

Follow-Up Phone Call

Date _____

Results _____
_____
_____

Interview

Date _____

Time _____

Interviewer _____
_____

Results _____

Thank-You Letter

Date _____
_____

Job Offer

Yes _____

No _____

Confirmation or "No Thank You, But" Letter

Date _____

Letter Type _____
_____

Résumé Mailing

Name _____

Title _____

Company _____

Address _____

Date Sent _____

Follow-Up Phone Call

Date _____

Results _____

_____

_____

_____

Interview

Date _____

Time _____

Interviewer _____

Results _____

Thank-You Letter

Date _____

_____

Job Offer

Yes _____

No _____

Confirmation or "No Thank You, But" Letter

Date _____

Letter Type _____

_____

Résumé Mailing

Name _____

Title _____

Company _____

Address _____

Date Sent _____

Follow-Up Phone Call

Date _____

Results _____

_____

_____

_____

Interview

Date _____

Time _____

Interviewer _____

Results _____

Thank-You Letter

Date _____

_____

Job Offer

Yes _____

No _____

Confirmation or "No Thank You, But" Letter

Date _____

Letter Type _____

_____

Winning Interview Techniques

8

The interview has been set up. Finally the efforts of your job campaign have come to fruition—you have been granted an interview. You know the time, the place, the importance of doing well. Suddenly you have an attack of nerves. You're both eager and anxious.

How will it go? Will you be able to convince the interviewer that not only can you do the job, but, indeed, you are absolutely the best person for it? You feel a little insecure. Will you be able to articulate your qualifications adequately?

What is happening to you happens to almost every job hunter: You're having a slight case of interview jitters. Don't worry; you're in good company. No matter how high up one is on the corporate ladder, being placed in the proverbial "hot seat" can be an unsettling experience. Our experience, as well as that of our colleagues all over the country, confirms that the great majority of job seekers find the interview the most stressful part of job hunting.

There are ways, however, of lessening that stress. The first step is to view the interview realistically. In most cases, job candidates tend to view the interview as an acid test of their abilities and self-worth. Such an attitude is extremely anxiety producing, and is guaranteed to elicit a negative response from the interviewer. But viewed realistically, the interview is simply a meeting between two equals—a buyer and a seller—to explore what each has to offer. Always keep in mind that feeling of equality between you and the interviewer.

The person conducting the interview is also under pressure. The interviewer must have the judgment to choose the most qualified candidate and must at the same time generate enough enthusiasm about the employer that when an offer is made, it will be accepted. Just as you are in competition with many other applicants, companies recruiting employees are similarly in competition with other employers trying to hire just the right person.

You were asked to be interviewed because some person in the company—an executive, an officer, the personnel director, or another representative of the employer—felt that the company's best interests would be served by knowing more about you. Your résumé generated interest in you. It indicated to them that you are qualified; now they are trying to determine if you are the *best* qualified.

With this in mind, you must now convince them that it is in their best interests to hire you. You must present yourself in such a manner that your assets and abilities are superior to any other candidate.

We are not surprised to find that the job does not always go to the most qualified person. It is possible to predict with a high degree of reliability which candidates will receive not one, but many job offers. We have analyzed the common denominator, the quality that these winners possess. It is that they give a first impression that projects honesty, sincerity, and enthusiasm. Given several candidates with virtually identical credentials, the job will almost invariably go to the individual projecting the most positive and enthusiastic image.

Creating The Right Impression

Because the very first impression you make will carry through the entire interview and greatly determine its outcome, it is of vital importance to create the most positive image possible. Your physical appearance, mannerisms, vocabulary, attitude, and nonverbal communication all contribute to the impression you make.

How do you convey the impression of sincerity? By being honest, open, and real. Simply by being yourself. Assume the attitude that the company wants you, and feel confident; this starts the self-fulfilling prophesy. *Feel* successful and chances are you *will* be successful.

Any form of role-playing that projects a personality other than your own is bound to lead to a disastrous interview. There is no way to predict what kind of person the employer is looking for and, if in fact you know, it is highly unlikely you could keep up the performance for the duration of the interview. Likewise, don't try to second guess an interviewer and tell him or her what you think they want to hear. It will almost always backfire.

Doing Your Homework

Because the interview is such a crucial part of the hiring process, take time to prepare yourself. This preparation will add to your self-confidence.

Your résumé will form the basis of the interview. No doubt, the interviewer will want you to elaborate upon some of the items you have mentioned only briefly. It is imperative that you review the résumé carefully before the interview. In fact, it is advisable to spend some time going over documentation, status reports, performance reviews, flow diagrams, or whatever you can in order to refresh your memory about previous projects or systems cited in your résumé. This will enable you to give specific technical details about your previous work, and demonstrate your thorough understanding of the system.

Many managers use the interview, not only as a way of

evaluating a candidate, but also to enhance their own technical background. After all, here you are, telling the interviewer that you've had experience, for example, with technical sales, especially a new engineering development. Just be sure you don't give wrong answers or guess at the answers to questions you're not sure of. You can never tell when the interviewer may, in fact, be a world class expert on just the type of product he or she is naively asking you to explain. If you don't know the answer to a technical question, just say so!

Managers become very suspicious if they ask for a technical explanation and get an evasive answer filled with generalities. Be sure to describe in detail any system design or marketing techniques you may have created or used which illustrate your particular contribution.

If you are seeking a management position, it will be valuable for you to learn as much as possible about the company conducting the interview. Find out whether it is a public or privately owned corporation. If listed in one of the major stock exchanges, find out how the stock is doing. Your broker may be able to give you insights into the history of the company.

In short, know the basic facts. The names of officers or partners, number of employees, and so on. Your local library is a source of such information. Directories such as *Standard & Poor's, Dun & Bradstreet*, and *Moody's* will also be extremely useful. The business periodical index will help you locate any recent press coverage. Spend some time reading current and back issues of trade journals that deal with the computer industry. It is possible you may come across an article referring to one of the companies that have invited you for an interview. Appearing up to date is an excellent method of scoring points.

Further Preparation

Make sure you organize your thoughts in advance to answer some of the tough questions which almost certainly come up during the interview process.

If you are between jobs, your reasons for leaving the last one will undoubtedly be probed during the interview. If presently employed, you will be asked the reasons you are seeking a new position. Preparing for these questions will provide you with the confidence you need to do your best. Always answer every question honestly. If you were fired, tell the simple truth. In these times of retrenchment, mergers, relocations, and layoffs, firing has become as familiar as television. Chances are that your prospective boss is no stranger to the experience, and will find it easy to empathize with you if you deal with the situation honestly.

If you were fired because your performance was in question, answer truthfully and try to transmit the extent to which you made this a learning experience. Never make any negative comments about a former staff member or your former or present employer.

More than likely you will be asked why you want to work for the company you are visiting. Again, be brief. Be also exact and direct. The research you have done about that particular employer will help you point out why you feel good about the interviewing company and how you can make a positive contribution to it. Wanting to move up, to earn a higher salary, to join a larger (or smaller) organization, having a desire to relocate; or wanting to make a career change—all these are appropriate reasons for looking for a new job. To sum it up, be as honest on your interview as you were on your résumé.

Asking Questions is Important, Too

Interviewers frequently pay as much attention to the questions candidates ask as to the answers they give. The questions you ask will serve as an indication of how much of the interviewer's information you have understood, and will show your level of competence and sophistication. Listen carefully and ask intelligent questions about the company. After all, you are also basing a decision about this job and this company on what you learn at the interview. Turn the interview into a true meeting of equals by politely, but firmly, asking the questions that are important to you.

Practice Questions

Though every interview is different, all will include questions requiring more than a "yes" or "no" answer. The interviewer will be listening not only for content, but for sincerity, poise, judgment, and ability to think quickly.

Spend some time before the interview developing answers to the following questions that you think might give you trouble. With a friend, husband, or wife—or even a tape recorder—go through each question. Prepare answers to give extemporaneously. There are no right or wrong answers. The purpose is to find out more about the subjective you. Aim for clarity, brevity, and, above all, honesty. Remember also that the actual wording and substance of these questions will vary to reflect the circumstances of each particular interview.

1. What do you consider to be your strong points?
2. What do you consider to be your weak points?
3. What motivates you?

4. What is your definition of success?
5. What did you enjoy most about your last job?
6. What did you like least about your last position?
7. Where would you like your career to be in five years?
8. What are your short-term career goals?
9. Do you prefer to work alone, or as part of a team?
10. How do you get along with your peers?
11. How good are you in motivating people?
12. To what magazines do you subscribe?
13. What newspapers do you read?
14. What were the last three books you read?
15. What are your hobbies?
16. How do you spend your leisure time?
17. Are you active in community affairs? If so, describe.
18. Why do you want to change jobs?
19. Why are you unemployed?
20. Why do you think you would be an asset to the company?
21. How well do you work under pressure?
22. How do you feel about working overtime?
23. Would you be willing to relocate to one of our branch offices? Would you be willing to travel?
24. How do you feel about working for a woman (man) or younger person?
25. What did you learn in your last position?
26. How did you get along with your boss on your last job?
27. How did you get along with the staff in your last job?
28. Why do you want to work for this company?
29. What do you consider your outstanding achievements?
30. What kinds of problems to you enjoy solving?
31. How often have you been ill in the past five years?
32. Are you willing to take a physical exam?
33. Are you willing to take a series of personality (aptitude) tests?
34. Have you ever been fired? If yes, why?
35. Do you have management ability? Describe.
36. How ambitious are you?
37. What was your last salary? What is your minimum salary at this time?

Salary Negotiation

It is the policy of most companies to conduct a series of interviews, because the employer is interested in the opinions of several members of the staff. This, of course, works both ways. It allows the applicant to learn more about the company—to decide if a rapport can be established with members of the firm and get first hand knowledge of working conditions in that particular company. In general, the more interviews you are invited to, the more seriously you are being considered.

Treat each individual interview with the same serious approach as the first. Always be prompt. It's a good idea to schedule no more than two interviews a day: one in the morning and another in the afternoon, since there is no way of telling how long an interview will last. Be a good listener, but feel free to ask any question that will be relevant.

Usually the question of salary will come up at the final or near final interview. Never begin salary negotiations until you are quite certain you have a job offer. In fact, don't bring up the subject of compensation; let the potential employer take the first step.

When asked about your present or last compensation package, answer concisely, including all bonuses and benefits. If you feel you were underpaid, mention that as one of the reasons for wanting to change jobs.

If you were referred to the employer by an employment agency or headhunter, it's a good idea to let them do the negotiating for you. Since they are very aware of market conditions and, in effect, will profit by your being hired, they will attack the question of compensation very vigorously. Their fee is usually based on a percentage of your salary, so it is in their best interest, as well as yours, to get the highest possible salary. Besides, as mentioned before, it's always helpful to have a third party negotiate for you.

If you are forced to do your own negotiating, stay flexible. If you know what salary range is being offered, put your salary expectations at the high end of the range. Remember, the interview is a screening process; if your requested minimum salary is considerably higher than the employer tends to pay, this could knock you out of the running.

Don't get boxed into a specific figure before you have to. Always talk in $5,000 to $10,000 ranges. If the interview has gone well and you are really interested in the company, aim high and then negotiate. Be sure to get all the relevant information concerning benefits: medical and dental insurance, profit-sharing plans, future salary increases, stock options, and so on. Consider all of the above as part of the total salary. If the subject of salary hasn't yet come up, and you are asked about your salary expectations, one approach is to answer the question with one of your own, "I'm glad you brought up the subject of compensation. What is the salary range for this job?" Give the employer a chance to give a figure, and then negotiate from there.

It's a good idea never to make a decision at the interview—whether it's the first, second and/or third interview. Ask for a few days or a week to think it over.

Thank the employer for the offer and indicate that you will give it serious consideration. Let them know when you will call back with your answer—no longer than a week or two. Bear in mind that the company will continue interviewing until the job has been filled, so don't delay too long. Give yourself just enough time to weigh any other offers and reflect more thoroughly on this one.

Sample Résumés

On the following pages you'll see a great many sample résumés. One of them may appeal to you as an example to follow. Even though parts of the samples, especially the job descriptions, may resemble what you wish to express, never copy them verbatim. These samples are included only to give you ideas that you can use to write your own résumé.

Use your completed worksheets, along with the form of the résumé you decide to use, and start writing. You will probably have to rewrite several times before you are completely satisfied with the results. Don't get discouraged!

Be sure to include all the pertinent information, and adhere to basic rules governing presentation and content. Here are some of those rules, the do's of writing a job-getting résumé.

1. Do keep it brief; one, or at the most, two pages.

2. Do choose a chronological style format; list your last or present job first, continuing in reverse chronological order.

3. Do place your name, address, and phone number in a conspicuous position on your résumé.

4. Do make sure your career objective (should you decide to use one) gives your résumé focus and is relevant to your experience and background.

5. Do list all dates of both employment and education history, leaving no unexplained gaps.

6. Do avoid long paragraphs; keep job descriptions under eight lines.

7. Do strengthen your résumé by using implied pronouns and action verbs.

8. Do use 8½ × 11-inch paper, preferably white or light color (beige, cream, buff, gray).

9. Do use one side of the page *only*; if two pages are used, be sure the sheets of paper are stapled together and your name is on each page.

10. Do make your résumé visually attractive—use plenty of white space, wide even-spaced margins, and clean crisp type.

11. Do proofread your résumé more than once. Make sure there are no misspellings, grammatical errors, or typos.

Sharon Cook Darrow
65 Elm Street
Kirkwood, Missouri 63122

Telephone: *(314) 653-2244*

JOB OBJECTIVE: Accountant

EXPERIENCE: Howell and Brooks, St. Louis, Missouri
1975-present   Accountant

Planned and organized own work under some supervision from the Group Manager. Assisted in determining the classifications, distribution and recording of accounting data.

Reconciled discrepancies in subsidiary ledgers and made proper adjustments. Assisted in the preparation of standardized accounting reports and statements of limited scope. Analyzed and interpreted statements and reports.

1972-1975   Koehler Manufacturing Company, St. Louis, Missouri
Accounting Clerk

Handled basic accounting transactions, coded invoices for proper distribution, classified transactions and processed warehouse invoices.

Education   B.S. degree - Community College, St. Louis, Missouri
1972

References   On request

Dorothy Gilmore, C.P.A.
312 W. 32nd Street
N.Y.C., NY 10031

Residence: (212) 814-2235   Office: (212) 787-3400

WORK EXPERIENCE

Barton, Klein & Dodd, CPA's.   June 1979 - Present
New York, NY 10007

   Senior Accountant

   · Preparation of income tax returns (Individual,
     Partnership, Corporation, etc.)
   · Preparation of financial reports and statements
   · Management advisory services for clients
   · Review and Compilation Services
   · Write up and general ledger work
   · Preparation of sales tax, commerical rent tax, and
     payroll tax returns
   · Responsible to develop and maintain accounting systems
     for clients
   · Responsible for whole engagements with limited
     supervision

EDUCATIONAL AND PROFESSIONAL ACCREDITATION:

   Certified Public Accountant, New York, 1981
   Bachelor of Business Administration - Accounting
        Columbia University, 1980
   Dean's List; elected to Beta Gamma Sigma
   Graduated Summa Cum Laude

PROFESSIONAL AFFILIATIONS:

   American Institute of Certified Public Accountants
   New York State Society of Certified Public Accountants
   Columbia University Alumni Association

REFERENCES:

   Furnished upon request

Patrick J. O'Mara
45 Hunter Lane
Grand Rapids, Michigan 49505
(616) 432-0146

Job Objective: **Accountant**

<u>**Experience**</u>   Millbank Furniture Company, Grand Rapids, Michigan

1982-1988   **Statistical Specialist** - Prepared detailed financial records including status reports, current and historical reports. Prepared journal entries, maintained records for marketing expenditures and inventories. Processed warehouse invoices and prepared sales reports.

1977-1982   **Accounts Receivable Analysis Clerk** - Made nonstandardized journal entries, coded invoices for proper accounting routing. Analyzed details of regular accounts. Assisted and trained other accounting clerks.

1975-1977   Walker Lumber Company, Inc., Grand Rapids, Michigan

              Cash Accounting Clerk - Performed various routine and nonroutine bookkeeping and basic accounting tasks including journal entries, verifying data and reconciling discrepancies, preparing detailed reports from raw data, and checking accounting documents for completeness, mathematical accuracy and consistency.

1973-1975   **Accounting Clerk Trainee** - Operated electronic calculator to make and verify computations. Prepared journal vouchers, entered postings, and filled in standard records and reports. Acquired a working knowledge of such accounting office procedures as posting and balancing, compiling data, preparing summaries, and verifying routine reports by checking against related details and previous data to reconcile irregularities.

<u>**Education**</u>   Community College—Currently enrolled in a statistics course and completed a two-semester course in mathematics.

              Lakewood Business School—Completed courses in basic accounting principles, intermediate accounting, 1973.

<u>**References**</u>   On request.

MICHAEL M. DANKO
1233 Ravan Park Avenue
White Plains, New York 10625
(914) 332-2277

JOB OBJECTIVE: Accounting/Finance with management possibilities

EXPERIENCE:

July 1982 to   Mitchell and Kern
  Present   Certified Public Accountants
                  14 Canal Street
                  New York, New York 10003

                  SENIOR ASSISTANT ACCOUNTANT

Employed as a staff accountant to perform basic functions on audit
engagements.

Within two years of employment, promoted to senior assistant accountant
with substantial raise in salary. Work involved increased responsibilities on audits and supervision over staff accountants.

Experienced in various types of commercial audit engagements such as
audits of manufacturing companies, import/export companies, brokerage
engagements, banks, and government contractors.

Received exposure in the areas of report drafting, financial statement
preparation and analytic review of operations.

EDUCATION: B.S. Accounting, Columbia University - 1982

                  References will be forwarded on request.

Karen Johnson
1452 North Hill St.
Beechwood, Ohio 44416
(513) 621-4133

EDUCATION: Harvard University, Bachelor of Science in
              Economics. Major: Accounting. May 1981.

              Barnard College 1977-1979
              Course of study as above.

CAREER AFFILIATIONS

     Haskins & Sells, Certified Public Accountants,
     Beechwood, Ohio.
          Senior Certified Public Accountant 9/81-Present.
          Professional supervisory experience in oil & gas
          tax shelters, industrial publishing, legal
          profession, retail, post-production video
          services. Primary responsibilities in planning,
          supervising, and reviewing audit engagements
          through completion of engagement. Experienced in
          corporate taxes, accounting systems analysis,
          internal control evaluations, computer system
          controls, consolidations, financial analysis,
          special projects in bankruptcy reporting as
          accountants for the trustee, and overall
          investigations of client systems for the purpose
          of improving operations and efficiency. Continuing
          professional education courses in Accounting &
          Auditing I, II, & III, Bankruptcy, Taxes, Written
          & Oral Communications & Investment Analysis.

     Deutch & Green, Certified Public Accountants, New York,
     NY
          Staff accountant 6/80-9/80. Staff accountant for
          audit of Shearson/American Express Company. Audit
          responsibilities included footnote disclosure
          preparation, security & exchange memberships, &
          cash.

     Career Placement Service, Harvard University 9/79-6/80
          Assistant to the Director of student career
          planning & corporate placement.

     United States Navy Active Duty, Midshipman 6/79-9/79
          Training in leadership, technical aspects of
          Surface Command, Submarine, Flight, and Marine
          Operations.

     United States Navy Active Duty, Midshipman 6/78-9/78

                                              (Continued)

Training at Naval Education Training Center,
Newport, R.I.

Information & Referral Service, Barnard College 9/77-
6/79
Public Relations Service for dignitaries,
corporate & academic officials visiting Cornell
University.

HONORS & AWARDS:

Dean's List, Barnard College & Harvard University
College Scholar Outstanding Academic Award, Barnard,
1977-79
Naval Reserve Officer Training Corps Scholarship 1977-
79
Fifty-five scholarships awarded to women on
national basis.
National Sojourner's Award Outstanding Sophomore,
Barnard, 1978-79
Mobil Oil Corporation Collegiate Competition Finalist

PROFESSIONAL STATUS & ASSOCIATIONS:

Certified Public Accountant, November 1981, New York
State
Harvard University Alumni Association

REFERENCES: Available upon request

Carla Johnson
124 White Drive
Sommers, NY 11416
(914) 968-3391
(914) 244-2000

WORK EXPERIENCE:
Career Blazers Temporary Personnel, White Plains, NY

1986 - Present

Junior Accountant
Preparation of monthly sales analysis and incentive bonus calculations using Lotus. Analyze results to report directly to the Chief Financial Officer. Responsible for account analysis, carry forwards, bank reconciliations and journal entries necessary to close the month on a timely basis.

Accounts Payable Clerk
Reconciled vendor accounts whenever there was a discrepancy. Supervised and trained new employees. Coded incoming vendor invoices.

1985 - 1986

ABC Corporation, Harrison, NY

Accounts Receivable Clerk
Verified accuracy of the daily accounts receivable book. Assisted Reporting Manager in preparation of monthly sales analysis. Prepared accounts receivable checks for deposit. Applied payments to receivable balances using the IBM System 38 computer. Entered adjustments to complete the breakdown of cash entries, as well as to eliminate the uncleared charge-backs.

1981 - 1983

Aetna INsurance Company, Hempstead, NY

Office Manager
Managed divisional office in addition to handling customer service for the area. Extensive supervision of trainees with regard to phone sales, customer price quotes, and in-house computer usage.

EDUCATION:
Nassau Community College
Degree: Associate in Applied Science - 1985
Major: Accounting

REFERENCES:
Available upon request.

GREGORY T. PHILIPS

108-43 Homelawn Street
Jamaica, New York 11432

(212) OL7-8843

Objective:
Challenging position in business management that will allow the opportunity to gain experience in the accounting and finance functions of a large company.

Education:
1985-present
Monroe College, Yonkers, New York
Currently enrolled in program leading to an M.B.A. Area of concentration is in financial management with special emphasis on the study of accounting for management control.

1981-1985
University of Fairfield, Fairfield, Connecticut
B.S. Major in Real Estate and Urban Economic Development. Extensive course work in real property appraisal and investment analysis.

Employment:
1/86-present
Monroe College, Yonkers, New York
Assistant to the manager of analytical studies. (Six-week internship.) Collected and synthesized price data for College's annual inflation study. Project involved library research as well as telephone contact with college suppliers. Internship led to current part-time position of coordinating draft for final report.

9/85-12/85
Eaton Real Estate, New Canaan, Connecticut
Real estate salesperson. Employed part-time by Eaton for the purpose of buying and selling real property.

9/83-9/85
University of Fairfield, Fairfield, Connecticut
Head resident. Responsible for running all aspects of a college dormitory. Duties included supervising residents, kitchen and maintenance staff and preparing all paperwork for Department of Student Affairs. Job was concurrent with full-time academic study to earn seventy percent of college expenses.

Summers:
Monroe College, Yonkers, New York
Dispatcher: Employed by physical plant department with responsibility for keeping accurate records on thirty-vehicle motor pool.

Groundsperson: Responsible for maintenance of college buildings and grounds.

References:
Available upon request.

Harvey Seller

110 Lakeview Drive
Chicago, IL 61245

(213) 769-4145

ACCOUNTANT/FINANCIAL MANAGER

with diversified public accounting, tax preparation and financial
management experience,
seeks a position in financial management.

**professional
experience**

1975 –
present

A. H. Shapiro & Co., CPA's, Chicago, IL
Manager

Directs the activities of semi-senior and staff
accountants in the conduct of certified audits for
a diverse clientele. Responsibilities include
audit planning, supervision of the audit and
direct communication with top management of client
companies.

· Participated in the conversion of a manual to
computerized billing system resulting in a more
efficient operation.

· Reviews audit results and confers with
management of client companies regarding financial
and operational weaknesses.

· Oversees the firm's tax planning activities.

· Assumed financial management responsibility
for a client in the real estate construction
business. Designed and implemented all internal
systems, recruited, hired, and trained personnel
and converted an existing manual system to an
automated one. On a continuing basis, reviews
company's financial results and makes appropriate
recommendations.

· Assisted a client in the publishing industry
in the development of a budgeting and forecasting
system. Subsequently, participated in negotiations
to sell the company to a publicly held company.

· For another publisher, computerized all
financial systems--accounts payable, receivable,

(Continued)

general ledger, payroll, subscription fulfillment
and distribution. Concurrently, revamped systems
resulting in increased cash flow and controls.

Joined company as a semi-senior accountant.
Participated in the conduct of certified audits in
the service and manufacturing industries.
Responsibilities included the preparation of
corporate, partnership and individual taxes on the
federal, state and local levels.

1973 – 1975	Koltman, Portnoy & Cohen, CPA's, Chicago, IL Semi-Senior Accountant

Joined this medium-size accounting firm as junior
accountant. Promoted to Accountant and then Semi-
Senior Accountant.

education	M.S., Taxation--University of Chicago, Chicago, IL B.S., Accounting--University of Chicago, Chicago, IL
references	Personal and professional references available on request.

Edward T. Washington
48-01 129th Street
New York, New York 10021
(212) 794-2376

OBJECTIVE:	Junior Accountant/Auditor Trainee
EDUCATION:	Hunter College, B.B.A. 1986 - Major: Public Accounting York Community College, A.A. 1984 - Major: Business Administration
GENERAL BACKGROUND:	Five years' professional experience utilizing customer relations and general accounting principles with the following firms:

Adjustments   Banker's Trust Co., New York, N.Y. 1984-Present

Accounts   Western Union Co., New York, N.Y. 1981-1983

SPECIFIC EXPERIENCE:

Adjustments   Inscribing amounts on checks from different branches of banking established throughout United States; balancing customer accounts by keeping accurate records of payments and adjustments; exacting time-keeping records and forwarding to payroll division.

Accounts   Processing and recording Western Union accounts including heavy customer contacts; keeping daily records of accounts receivable; acting as liaison between customer and accounting division; disseminating general information into specific codes for business purposes involving written correspondence and interpretative designs.

COLLATERAL COURSES:

Law, Management Science, Computer Information Science, Marketing, Business Management, Calculus, Statistics, Financial Analysis, Individual Taxation, Partnership Corporation Taxes, Estates and Trusts, Electronic Data Processing, and Advanced Professional Auditing (one year). Advanced Accounting practice. Seminar in Accounting, Specialized Accounting.

REFERENCES: Available upon request.

SYLVIA SLATER
340 Slate Street
San Francisco, California 81416
(219) 765-2448
(219) 899-6400

EMPLOYMENT HISTORY

7/87 - Present	The Dalton School

Admissions Representative

- Responsible for meeting weekly student application goal
- Had highest close ratio of applications to interviews
- Interviewed and followed up on over 250 students
- Dealt with guidance counsellors to obtain transcripts for student evaluation
- Managed my enrollment of over 150 students
- Held financial plans for my student enrollment via computer analysis
- Maintained and monitored enrolled students' tuition payments

9/85 - 7/87   Hill & Rogers, Inc.
Executive Recruiter

- Counselled, interviewed and qualified candidates
- Obtained candidates and clients via telephone solicitation and referrals
- Trained and supervised two recruiters
- Client contacts included: Banking, Brokerage, Marketing and Financial Services Advertising

4/85 - 9/85   Stern & Stern, Inc.
Placement Counselor/Personnel Consultant

- Screened, interviewed and advised candidates for clerical and/or non-exempt positions
- Assisted in resume writing
- Solicited new accounts
- Counselled applicants on interview techniques

8/83 - 4/85   Manning, Selvage & Lee Public Relations
Account Coordinator

- Executed special events
- Planned press conferences
- Obtained contacts in broadcast and print media
- Wrote press releases

EDUCATION   Ohio University
BA, Public Communications; 5/83

REFERENCES   Available upon request

DIANE LEVITT
18 Anderson Ave.
Queens, NY 12416

(718) 889-9106
(212) 884-2240

EMPLOYMENT EXPERIENCE

October 1981 - Present: FRANK BRYOIER & SONS, INC.
ADMINISTRATIVE ASSISTANT

Work for three principals, prepare confidential reports, compile
agendas, schedule travel plans, screen correspondence, coordinate
business appointments, maintain filing system, plan annual office
parties, prioritize and distribute work, in charge of
computerized accounts receivable for two companies, secretarial
duties including Multimate word processing, fax machine, telex,
billing and order entries, heavy phone contact with clients.

March 1979 - August 1981   BAKER, TODD & BAKER, INC.
EXECUTIVE SECRETARY/
ADMINISTRATIVE ASSISTANT

Word processing, typing all specifications, correspondence and
expense reports as well as making all travel arrangements. In
charge of job scheduling and directly involved in contract
preparation. Secretary for fifty draftsmen along with three
immediate supervisors and four department managers. Heavy phone
and personal contact with clients.

July 1977 - February 1979:   HILL & BARRON'S
SECRETARY

Secretary for three principals within three different high volume
jewelry firms. Duties included typing bills and correspondence
and having an operating knowledge of computerized accounts
receivable. Telex operator. Heavy phone and personal contact with
clients.

May 1975 - July 1977:   OTIS & MEYERS, INC.
RECEPTIONIST

Receptionist for jewelry firm. Typed correspondence and assisted
shipping department. CRT operator - input all billing and
shipping information.

EDUCATION

September 1971 - June 1974:   SIENNA COLLEGE, BRONX, N.Y.

References furnished upon request.

ELLEN A. BRZOWSKI
81 St. Marks Place
New York, New York 10037

(212) 559-9630

VICTOR TEMPORARIES (1982-To Date)
  New York, New York

Assistant to President
Interview applicants
Liaison with clients
Telephone sales
Bookkeeping

AMERICAN MOTORS CORPORATION (1979-1982)
  White Plains Zone Office

Assistant Office Manager (Government Bonded)
Responsible for:
Expense accounts for - sales representatives,
district managers and all zone office personnel.
Travelletter authorizations.
Accident reports.
Accounts payable and receivable.
Zone sundry reports for car distribution.
'Parts' account for twenty-eight General Motors
dealers.

REVLON (1975-1978)
  New York Office

Supervisor of Order Department
Responsible for:
Liaison with cosmetic buyers of superior store chains.
Supervised eight members of staff.
Organized promotional material for new items.
In charge of setting up new accounts.

MARTIN CARPETS (1973-1975)
  Brookfield, Connecticut

Assistant Manager
Customer relations
Sales representative
New accounts establishment   (Continued)

Ellen A. Brzowski

(<u>Personal</u>)

Yorktown Teachers College (1971-1973)
A.S. Business Administration

_____

References will be furnished on request.

DEAN ASHER

Address

49 W. Mangnot Lane
Easton, Vt. 05341

Telephone

Home: 919-619-0936
Service: 914-616-0319

Work Experience

1984-present: Researcher/Technical Editor,
Lipcot-Abbey-McLoyton-Thomas-McCarthy-
Stratton (Engineers and Architects), 345 Park
Avenue, New York, Department of Environmental
Planning and Socioeconomic Studies. Assembled
information concerning complicated and
sensitive subject matter through personal
contacts; researched documents, statutes and
governmental procedures; set style and
format; edited and proofread environmental
impact statements and proposals.

1984: Assistant publicity director, Mainman
Ltd., 405 Park Avenue, New York. Assisted
with ad campaigns, preparation of press kits,
news releases, publicity events and planning
of Times Square spectacular billboard for RCA
recording artists.

1983: Reporter/Ad Salesman, The Lower Cape,
Provincetown, Massachusetts. Covered local
news stories for shoppers' guide and local
news weekly publication.

1982: Customer Service, U.S. Committee for
UNICEF, 331 Easton Street, Easton, Vermont.
Responsible for personal correspondence
concerning customer complaints and orders in
the greeting card program.

1978-1982: Journalist, U.S. Navy. Aboard an
LST in Vietnam, inaugurated a campaign of
hometown news releases and stories of
shipboard life with the riverine forces in
the Mekong Delta. Public Affairs Office,
Third Naval District Headquarters, San Jose.
Wrote news releases, photographed and
organized mass media command presentations,
press contact at official ceremonies and
admiral's aide at social engagements.

Education

Department of Defense

(Continued)

Information School (DINFOS)
Fort Harrison, Indiana

Northwestern University
National High School Institute
Evanston, Illinois

Graduate, 1978
Journalism/Public Relations

Graduate, 1976
Speech/Drama

Honors   Alternate Delegate to the World Youth
Assembly, 1980.
United Nations, New York City

Organizations   Executive Secretary for the Neighbors of
Teilson Park, YMCA.

Recommendations furnished upon request.

Rose J. Martinson
43 Racine Avenue
Skokie, Illinois 60076

(312) 546-7898

Job Objective:
Administrative Assistant

Experience	Howard T. Mack, Inc.	Skokie, Illinois

1980-present   Assistant to the president and owner of this firm dealing in rare coins and stamps. The president, who travels extensively, is primarily concerned with purchasing large collections and negotiating financial transactions involving the expansion of company operations through new investments.

Responsible for employment, training, salary administration, and terminations for 150 employees. Supervisor of four departments: bookkeeping, shipping, direct mail sales, and customer relations. Determine adjustments and credits on customer transactions. Responsible for the monthly distribution of want lists to over 300 dealers. Determine bid and purchase price on coins and stamps from private collections.

1976-1980	The Field Foundation	Chicago, Illinois

Assistant to Director of Office Services. Supervised office staff of thirty clerical, stenographic, and machine operator personnel. Interviewed applicants, trained new employees, scheduled work assignments, and made equipment changes to improve efficiency.

1973-1976	Northwestern University	Chicago, Illinois

Assistant to Placement Director. Job searched and placed undergraduate students in part-time jobs. Met with recruitment representatives from industry and arranged interviews for them with students who were completing graduate work. For the first two years in this capacity, performed routine clerical and secretarial tasks.

Education   Northwestern University - A.B. degree, June 1973

History Major and Psychology Minor. Junior Class President.

References   On request.

ALVARO SUAREZ
40 West 72nd St.
New York, NY 10023
212-787-0871

EXPERIENCE

1984–
1989

Personal Secretary to First Secretary of Dominican Republic to the United Nations, New York. Handled all personal correspondence, prepared all details for major international sports events in Dominican Rep., arranged housing and entertainment for dignitaries visiting Mission to the U.N. Acted as interpreter.

1981–
1984

Administrative Assistant and Secretary, ANCO International, New Jersey. Served in this capacity to President of this corporation. Assumed responsibility for office in his absence, including handling of all correspondence, translations in Spanish and Italian, transcribing of large volume of shorthand as well as dictaphone-typing; made arrangements for hotel accommodations and booked space for conferences, both domestic and overseas. Acted as interpreter for foreign company representatives visiting New York.

1980–
1981

Executive Secretary to the Director of International Operations, Standard Tobacco International, New York. Handled all press contacts, translated foreign press releases, assumed all secretarial responsibilities, and assisted in all public relations activities.

1975–
1980

Executive Secretary/Assistant Fashion Coordinator, Longine-Pioneer Corporation, New York. Translated fashion copy for magazines and newspapers, prepared press parties, fashion shows, performed secretarial duties.

EDUCATION
B.A. in Social Studies, 1975—University of Santo Domingo, Dominican Republic

LANGUAGES
Fluency in Spanish, Italian, English

SECRETARIAL SKILLS
Typing: 85 wpm;   Steno: 90 wpm.   Dictaphone

REFERENCES
On request

NAME: David R. Chosack

ADDRESS: 987 Chicago Street
             St. Louis, Missouri 63101
             (314) 548-4375

EXPERIENCE:

<u>Kenyon and Eckhardt, Inc.</u> April 1979-June 1988. Hired as Account Coordinator for Air France, Helena Rubinstein, and Foreign Vintage accounts. In addition to the regular duties, other responsibilities as coordinator were to check the monthly production invoices prior to their submission to the client and to insure that an ad was released to a publication for every insertion placed on a media estimate. The Anaconda, French West Indies Tourist Board, Royal Air Maroc, and Alfred Dunner accounts were added to the coordinating assignments.

<u>In March 1982</u>, promoted to Account Executive on Air France account. During past three years gained experience in supervising all facets of the account. In detail, this included initiating and approving overall campaigns, writing copy, planning media, and complete supervision of print, radio, and TV production.

<u>Doyle Dane Bernbach, Inc.</u> June 1976-April 1979. Hired specifically to traffic portions of the Monsanto account in TV and print. Handled these portions until February 1967, then was transferred to the tire and corporate divisions of Uniroyal (TV and print). During this time, also assisted with traffic on Sony, portions of Burlington Industries and other house accounts. Subsequently, the shoe and golf ball divisions of Uniroyal and American Tourister Luggage were added.

<u>McCall Corporation</u>. December 1972-June 1976. Position as Assistant Advertising Quality and Control Manager for production department of McCall's Magazine. Channeled flow of plates from various advertising agencies throughout the United States to our printing plant in time for each closing date of McCall's and Redbook magazines. Had gained experience in control of color quality as well as in the ordering of safety shells and electros.

<u>In January 1976</u>, promoted to the position of Advertising Traffic Manager. In this capacity had complete charge over the responsibilities listed above, in addition to supervising a small staff.

<u>Kaiser, Sedlow & Temple</u>. December 1971-December 1972. Started with Burke, Charles and Guignon Advertising as Traffic Manager. When agency merged with Kaiser, Sedlow & Temple in June 1962, continued as Traffic Manager and Media Director on Twentieth Century Fox, Columbia Pictures, Embassy Pictures, and Arco Lighting.

(Continued)

David R. Chosack - Page 2

Compton Advertising Agency. August 1970-October 1971. Started as messenger in traffic department and gradually assisted Traffic man with accounts such as Kelly-Springfield and some Proctor and Gamble Company products.

EDUCATION: Queens and City Colleges 1968-1970

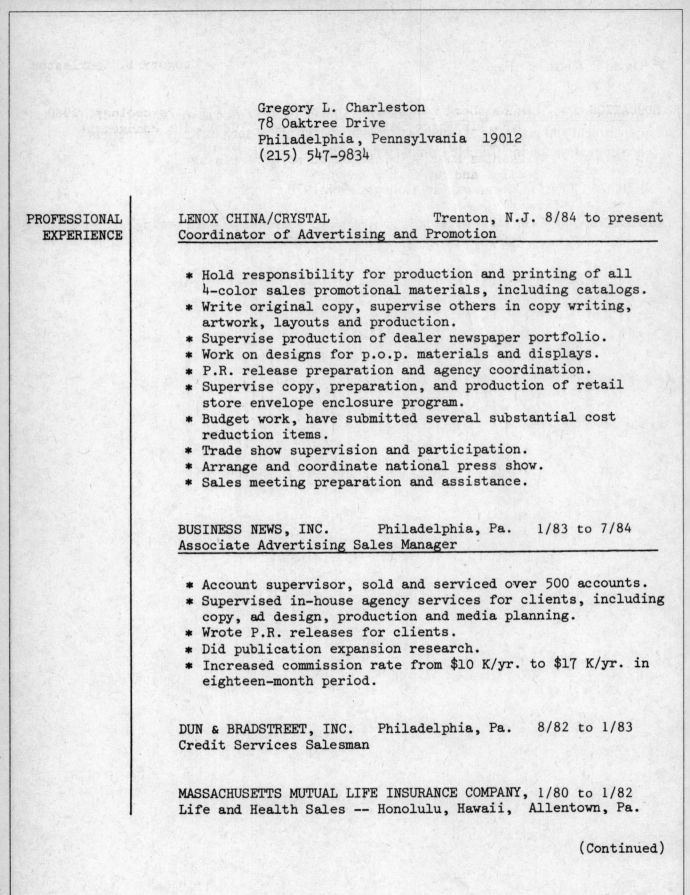

Gregory L. Charleston
78 Oaktree Drive
Philadelphia, Pennsylvania 19012
(215) 547-9834

**PROFESSIONAL
EXPERIENCE**

LENOX CHINA/CRYSTAL   Trenton, N.J. 8/84 to present
Coordinator of Advertising and Promotion

* Hold responsibility for production and printing of all
  4-color sales promotional materials, including catalogs.
* Write original copy, supervise others in copy writing,
  artwork, layouts and production.
* Supervise production of dealer newspaper portfolio.
* Work on designs for p.o.p. materials and displays.
* P.R. release preparation and agency coordination.
* Supervise copy, preparation, and production of retail
  store envelope enclosure program.
* Budget work, have submitted several substantial cost
  reduction items.
* Trade show supervision and participation.
* Arrange and coordinate national press show.
* Sales meeting preparation and assistance.

BUSINESS NEWS, INC.   Philadelphia, Pa.   1/83 to 7/84
Associate Advertising Sales Manager

* Account supervisor, sold and serviced over 500 accounts.
* Supervised in-house agency services for clients, including
  copy, ad design, production and media planning.
* Wrote P.R. releases for clients.
* Did publication expansion research.
* Increased commission rate from $10 K/yr. to $17 K/yr. in
  eighteen-month period.

DUN & BRADSTREET, INC.   Philadelphia, Pa.   8/82 to 1/83
Credit Services Salesman

MASSACHUSETTS MUTUAL LIFE INSURANCE COMPANY, 1/80 to 1/82
Life and Health Sales -- Honolulu, Hawaii, Allentown, Pa.

(Continued)

EDUCATION   Muhlenberg College, Allentown, Pa., B.A. in Psychology, 1980
                 U.S. Air Force Telecommunications-Electronics Management
                 School
                 Charles Morris Price School of Advertising
                 Sales and Marketing Schools

OBJECTIVE   Growth-oriented position in advertising-marketing.
                 References provided by request.

Maria Zawacki
68 Old Mill Road
Springfield, Michigan 48678
(313) 821-9641

Job Objective:	To function as airline reservationist or reservations supervisor.

Experience

4/79-present	**Reservationist**, Great North Airlines, Detroit, Mich. Make reservations for GN Airlines to all locations in United States and Canada; arrange connecting flights, teletype and receive information.
7/70-4/79	**Reservationist**, Trans-West Airlines, Chicago, Ill. Performed all reservation duties at O'Hare Airport; arranged connecting flights; type and teletype; operated small computer.

Education

June 1970	Graduated from Laverne Bell Modeling School, Chicago, Ill.
June 1969	Commercial Diploma Mother Seton High School, Chicago, Ill.

References

Full references will be furnished on request.

WILLIAM A. ELLIOTT

20 Jerome Drive
Putnam Lake
Patterson, N.Y. 12563

EDUCATION

1972-1975, School of Visual Arts, 209 E. 23rd Street, New York, New York. Graduated with Associates Degree.

EMPLOYMENT

10/80-present — For the past five years worked for the New York Zoological Society as a Designer-Illustrator. During the last two years held a supervisory position as the assistant Art Director. Duties included designing of all printed material used for the Zoo and Aquarium. (Annual reports, educational brochures, books, posters, letterheads, logos.) Was also involved in the design and production of all the educational graphics that appear both outside and inside the buildings. All of the above mentioned work was designed and produced on the Zoo's property.

Additional experience — Three years' experience operating a 20 × 24 Chemco copy camera. Five years experience silk screening multicolor back-lit graphics.

1/79-10/80 — R. H. Macy's — Advertising. Worked freelance for Macy's designing all advertising for 22 departments such as Cosmetics, Jewelry, Children's Apparel, Sporting Goods, etc.

1976-1978 — U. S. Army. Worked as Post Illustrator at Ft. Richardson, Alaska, during which time designed displays for A.U.S.A. Convention held in Washington, D.C. in September, 1966. Also worked on the designing and construction of displays used in the commemoration of the Alaskan Centennial. Transferred to White Sands Missile Range, New Mexico, where worked on several Army promotional displays.

Bill Elliott wildlife illustrator
animal portraits wildlife illustration birds•fish•mammals 914-279-9338

CONSTANCE ANITA KRAVITZ
456 Philadelphia Road
Camden, New Jersey 08705

BUSINESS EXPERIENCE

Electronics Age Magazine
CHILTON PUBLISHING COMPANY

1981 to present   Assistant Art Director - March 1973 to present
Report to Art Director and Managing Editor.
Responsibilities include art selection and preparation, illustrating, magazine layout, and some cover
design. When necessary, act as a Chilton representative at our printer's and serve in a supervisory
capacity. Position involves heavy contact with
artists, writers, editors, and suppliers and the
ability to work under tight deadlines.

Production Editor - November 1981 to March 1983
Responsible for all copy flow on Electronics Age.
Programmed software on Typeset 8 system for computer
typesetting. Served as liaison between art and
editorial departments and between the printer, various
vendors and the magazine. Completed a work flow
analysis/time-motion study to determine more efficient
production processes which recently resulted in a re-
allocation of personnel.

GREYSTONE PUBLISHING (Franson Corporation)

June 1981 to   Production - Position included responsibility for the
November 1981   design and layout of decorating encyclopedias. Was
working art director for a short time before leaving.
Much work done in the area of paste-up and mechanicals,
line drawings, type spacing and other duties involving
direct mail pieces.

DAN RIVER MILLS

January 1981   Commercial Artist - Originated fabric design on hand
to June 1981   loom.

(Continued)

2   Constance Anita Kravitz

THE TEXAS CATHOLIC NEWSPAPER   Dallas, Texas

January 1979   Staff Artist - Job entailed complete responsibility for
to January 1981 all art work associated with the paper itself and its
                 advertising. Also estimated the amount of advertising
                 and editorial copy per issue and determined the forms
                 accordingly. Designed cover and produced the Diocesan
                 Directory for 1971.

September 1988   HUNTER COLLEGE   C.C.N.Y.
to present   Studio and Art History Major/English minor

September 1975   UNIVERSITY OF DALLAS   Irving, Texas
to June 1977   Fine Arts Major

MORRIS LEVINE
21 East 50th Street
New York, New York 10017
(212) 966-0561

OBJECTIVE: Growth position that would effectively utilize
my experience as commercial artist.

EXPERIENCE

1981-present   <u>Art Director</u>, Schirmer Graphics Company. Create original art for audio-visual shows and slide production, mechanicals for annual report
production, and photography.

1976-1981   <u>Assistant Art Director</u>, Grosset Publications, Inc.
Circulation Art Department. Created direct mail pieces, sales aids
promotions, product ads, rate cards, logos and letterheads, 4-color
brochures, spot drawings and slides, from concept to completion.

1971-1976   <u>Assistant Art Director</u>, Creative Arts Magazine Enterprises. Created
sales aids promotions, direct mail pieces, product ads, research
studies, rate cards, brochures, logos and letterheads, inserts, rough
and semi-comps.

1969-1971   <u>Assistant Art Director</u>, Mechanical Designs Magazine. Emphasis on
general boardwork, layout, mechanicals, photo cropping and scaling,
spot drawings.

1967-1969   <u>Staff Artist</u>, Clint Crafts Publishers, Art Department. General boardwork, layout, mechanicals, photo cropping and scaling.

EDUCATION

Industrial Arts High School - Graduated June, 1967, Commercial Arts Diploma.

REFERENCES

Furnished upon request.

JOYCE PETERS
14 State Street
Albany, NY 12415
(313) 876-1266
(313) 875-5000

CAREER OBJECTIVE: To secure a responsible position with a progressive firm that will utilize my skills and experience and provide growth opportunities.

BUSINESS EXPERIENCE

Dec. 1981 - Present
St. Martin's Press
100 Center Lane
Albany, NY

Feb. 1985 - Present
Position:
ART AIDE

Responsibilities:
Responsible for trafficking of illustrations, mechanicals, and art layout between printers and compositors for new publications.
Maintenance of departmental photo files. Also included in my duties are phone work, filing, light typing of departmental correspondence, and maintain freelance ledger. Input data to effect update of inventory files on CRT. Create document files and data processing on Wang system.

Position:
ILLUSTRATION EXPEDITOR

Responsibilities:
Responsible for preparing, organizing, and expediting all material that flows between compositors and printers. Responsible for working with production department to obtain dummy request. Recordkeeping in departmental log files. Preparation of materials for paste-ups and layout requests.

Nov. 1980 - Nov. 1981
300 E. 4th st.
Albany, NY
Albany Youth Council

Position:
CLERICAL OFFICE ASSISTANT

Responsibilities:
General office duties, including but not limited to filing, phone work, operation of all office equipment, including copiers, adding machines, and photostat cameras.

EDUCATION

Sept. 1974-June 1977
Albany High School

REFERENCES
AVAILABLE UPON REQUEST

MARJORIE
TARKINGTON

PROFESSIONAL HISTORY

March 1987
to present

Art Director
Marcia James Assoc., Miami, FL
Develop visual concepts to produce
thumbnails, comps, and mechanicals for ads,
brochures, press kits, direct mail packages,
logos, and sales sheets. Direct studio and
location photography. Commission and
supervise illustrators. Interface with
clients to obtain information and advance the
creative process. Oversee print production
including blueprint and color-key o.k.'s, and
press approvals. Supervise graphic designer
and freelance mechanical artists.

January 1986
to March 1987

Assistant Art Director
Stern's & Co., Miami, FL
Designed 4-color catalogs, weekly tabloids,
ads, and store graphics for more than thirty
major retail stores. Assisted Art Director
with catalog production: layout, comps, type
specification, and mechanicals. Coordinated
merchandise samples. Supervised fashion and
product photography. Created corporate
graphic materials.

January 1985
to January 1986

Freelance Graphic Designer
Designed ads, posters, brochures, and 4-color
catalogs. Clients:
    Deutch & Shea Advertising,
    Miami, FL
    American Council on the Teaching of
    Foreign Languages, Hastings-on-Hudson, NY

August 1983
to January 1985

Graphic Designer
The Daily Star, Miami, FL
Designed editorial pages. Created logos and
photo layouts for special advertising
sections. Created new advertising formats to
attract new advertisers. Designed new
publications New Men's News and The Women's
Registry.

September 1981
to July 1983

Graphic Designer
The Miami News, Miami, FL

Designed advertising, supplement covers, and
photo pages. Edited photos. Photographed news

(Continued)

events. Created and implemented weekly full page photo essays. Introduced and managed in-house graphic design firm.

July 1979
to July 1981

Freelance Fabric Designer
Designed and printed fabrics using Japanese dying techniques. Created "wearable art" costumes. Marketed garments through galleries and participated in major wearable art exhibitions.

EDUCATION

September 1983
to 1985

Graphic communications studies.
School of Visual Arts and Pratt Institute, New York, NY.

September 1980
to August 1981

Professional photography studies with Rae Russel, veteran magazine photographer. Focus on photo-journalism and portraiture.

September 1978
to June 1980

Master of Fine Arts Degree.
New York University

June 1978

Bachelor of Fine Arts degree.
New York University

16 California Ave., Miami, FL
(305) 815-8334

LAURIE ADAMS

ADDRESS
24 Oak Park Road
Peekskill, New York 11304
(914) 341-4416

EDUCATION
1981-1985: Brown University, B.A. Studio Art.
Includes study at Sir John Cass School of
Art, London, England, and Rhode Island School
of Design.

1980: Syracuse University, Photography and Art
Workshop.

EMPLOYMENT
1985-Present: General boardwork, Design Plus Inc.,
Yorktown Heights, N.Y.

1985-Summer: General boardwork, High Times
Magazine, New York, N.Y.

1982-Summer: Mechanical, paste-up artist, Lasky
Company Lithographers, Millburn, N.J.

1980-Summer: Art Instructor, Camp Rondack, N.Y.

**HONORS AND
AWARDS**
Salutatorian, Morristown High School.
First Prize, Art Contest, City Federal Bank.
Alumni Award, Morristown High School.
National Merit Scholarship Semi-Finalist.

REFERENCES
Available on request.

John Kassech
13-06 45th St.
L.I.C., NY 11106
(718) 929-1150

PROFESSIONAL EXPERIENCE:

1980-
present

Queens County District Attorney
Flushing, New York

Assistant District Attorney
    Trial litigation in major felony cases; extensive
motion practice; preparation and investigation of
homicides, sex crimes, and economic crimes;
vehicular homicide supervisor.

1978-
1980

Silverman and Saltman
New York, New York

Associate Attorney
    Civil trial litigations, contract negotiation;
antitrust and corporate law; Family Court and
marital proceedings; and arbitration.

EDUCATION:

Loyola University School of Law
New Orleans, Louisiana
J.D., 1978

New York University
New York, New York
B.A., 1975; Major in Sociology

BAR ADMISSIONS:

New York Bar Association
Florida Bar Association
United States Supreme Court
United States District Court
    Southern District of New York
    Eastern District of New York
United States Court of Appeals
    Sixth Circuit

References furnished upon request.

ELIZABETH MORRIS
169 Ninth Street
Milford, PA 18428
(717) 296-6215

BACKGROUND

Extensive experience in all legal aspects of real estate investments and corporate matters with management positions of increasing responsibility. In addition, eight years prime responsibility for the risk management insurance programs of a national company.

EXPERIENCE

Private Practice   **1985-1989**

Associated with Harris, Newman & Miller, specializing in commercial, corporate and real estate law.

State Farm Insurance Company   **1964-1984**

Vice President - Counsel and Assistant Secretary

Managed real estate investment division of Law Department, comprised of three attorneys and a paralegal assistant. Implemented and successfully completed fifteen real estate joint ventures in nine states within eighteen months. Completed negotiation and documentation for a unique joint venture condominium corporate headquarters. Consummated real estate investments on a national basis. Negotiated leases and brokerage agreements on owned properties and as tenant in national sales offices. Initiated and implemented errors and omissions insurance coverage for our national sales organization and the officers and directors of the company.

Associate Counsel

Conducted national corporate practice including real estate investments, litigation, construction contracts, leases, legislation, consumer protection, national marketing programs, and casualty insurance.

Esso Oil Company   **1961-1964**

Attorney (Law Department)

Maintained corporate practice including all phases of real estate. Responsible for anti-trust, product contracts, landlord and tenant, asset and stock acquisitions.

EDUCATION

Columbia College: B.S., Recommended for Fullbright Scholarship.

Columbia Law School: Admitted New York State Bar.

AFFILIATIONS

Pennsylvania County Lawyers Association: Secretary of Real Property Committee
American Bar Association
American Land Title Association
Association of Life Insurance Counsel

John Corwin
62 Pine Street
Scarsdale, New York 10583
(914) 823-1234

EXPERIENCE:

1/81-present   ASSOCIATE COUNCIL
       Sklar Paints, Inc.
       Yonkers, New York

       RESPONSIBILITIES:
       Trade regulation/restrictive business practices
       counseling. Monitor compliance with *FTC* Consent
       Decrees.
       Draft and review *contracts*, including: distributor-
       ships; licenses (patent, know-how, trademark);
       import/export; purchase and sale of goods, services,
       businesses; joint ventures; leases, realty, secrecy,
       employment; secured transactions.
       Negotiate warranty and product liability claims.
       Review with management foreign legal require-
       ments, and implement appropriate action.
       Coordinate litigation in conjunction with local
       trial counsel.
       Maintain corporate records for various subsidiaries.

EDUCATION: New York University
       Graduate School of Law
       LL.M., January 1981
       Class standing - Top Quarter

       New York Law School
       J.D. January 1980
       Class standing - Top Quarter

       Cornell University
       B.A. June 1977
       Class standing - Top Quarter

       References available upon request.

Ruth Levine
412 E. 72nd Street
New York, NY 10313
(212) 412-3150
(212) 415-6800

EDUCATION: MBA-Financial Management, Fordham University, 1980
BBA-Accounting, Fordham University, 1970

EXPERIENCE:

Sept 1982   Lord & Taylor, Inc.   Audit Manager
  to
Present   Responsibilities include analytical review and
verification of financial records and operating
controls. Developed audit programs, established
guidelines for physical distribution and
warehousing of inventory. An integral part of the
review was to evaluate the adequacy of internal
controls and the extent of compliance with
management policy. At audit completion, the
exceptions were discussed and an objective opinion
with remedial guidelines was submitted to
management.

Jan. 1978   Oxman Dry Cleaners, Inc.
  to
Aug. 1982   Operated family dry cleaning establishment,
engaged in all aspects of business activity
necessary to its daily operation. Maintained
financial records, performed purchasing and
accounting functions.

Jan. 1973   American Fabric, Inc.   Senior Auditor/EDP Auditor
  to
Dec. 1977   Conducted financial/operational audits of both
domestic and international facilities. The review
included an in-depth study of the manufacturing
process, evaluated and recommended changes in
policies concerning internal controls. Performed
EDP audits, familiar with computer control
applications on IBM sys/37 DOS. Knowledge of COBOL
and BASIC languages. Supervised and monitored
performance of three staff auditors. The review
provided management with assurance that effective
controls and policies were being administered.

July 1970   Haskins & Sells, C.P.A.   Jr. Accountant/Auditor
  to
Dec. 1972   Participated in certified audits of clients in
fields of banking, brokerage, hotels,
construction, and insurance. The review included
analysis, verification, and confirmation. Assisted
in preparing financial statements, SEC reports,
budgetary planning, and consolidations.

LANGUAGES: Fluent in Spanish and Italian

REFERENCES: Will be furnished upon request

Teresa Ortega
1852 Palm Springs Blvd.
Miami, Florida 33182
(305) 890-8342

Career Objective

To utilize my biochemical expertise
in the area of medical research.

Experience

<u>Biochemist</u>, South Florida Medical Center, 9/88-present.
Supervised staff of sixteen chemists, biologists and lab technicians.
Set up procedures for analysis of organic and inorganic compounds
for both quality and quantity. Was responsible for scheduling and
planning experiments, maintaining all records in laboratory manual; in charge of test animals, dissections, blood, tissue tests.

Education

M.S. Biology, Columbia University, 1988
B.S. Chemistry, Smith College, 1986

References on request

DONALD PAIGE

75 Shore Road
Houston, Texas 75213
(415) 225–4889
(415) 765–6644

OBJECTIVE: Active participation in company operations in ways that will enable me to contribute my skills and knowledge, and to provide an opportunity for professional development and career growth.

EXPERIENCE: Shaw and Sons Inc., Houston, Texas   June 1985–June1989
Position: ACCOUNTS RECEIVABLE, BOOKKEEPER
CREDIT & COLLECTION SUPERVISOR

Responsible for invoice processing daily and weekly. Checking service order changes and chargebacks. In charge of cash receipts posting to computer, maintained customer billing files, supervised and trained collection and customer service representatives. Responsible for monthly closings, aging report generation. Credit investigations on all new clients and new client credit limits. Monitored Dunn and Bradstreet reports for changing financial status on clients. Other duties: payroll EDP, Accounts Payable, Supervision.

BAYLOR INSTITUTE OF TECHNOLOGY   July 1982–April 1985
Department of Business and Finance, Atlanta, Georgia
Position: ACCOUNTING ASSISTANT
Departments: Payroll & Records/Grant & Contract Accounting

Duties: Accounts payable, accounts receivable, budget forecasting and revision modification for direct and indirect cost for federal grants and contracts awarded to the insitution. EDP Payroll bi-weekly processing for 54 different departments encompassing 700 + employees, via data entry to main frame.

SOFTWARE/   IBM PC XT/IBM 34 & 36/Data Media Excel 42/Textronics/Wang/
HARDWARE   Digital/Decwriter/Lotus 1, 2, 3,/Database III/Lanier Word Processor.

EDUCATION: Baylor University, 1985

REFERENCES: Available upon request.

Pablo Gonzalez
12 Prickly Pear Road
Santa Fe, New Mexico 87524
(505) 239-8765

POSITION OBJECTIVES
        Desire to be Manager or Assistant Manager of a
        dynamic Accounting Department or Division with
        opportunities to be Assistant Controller.

WORK HISTORY

    1983-present   Supervisor - Accounts Payable, White's, Santa
                    Fe. Supervise 5 people; process approx. 15 to
                    40 vendor adjustments and inquiries per day;
                    handle accruals and reconciliations both
                    quarterly and yearly.

    1980-1983   Manager - Accounts Payable, Quality Foods,
                    Santa Fe. Supervised 25 people; processed
                    approximately 600 invoices per day; audited
                    vendor invoices for payment; handled vendor
                    adjustments and inquiries.

    1970-1980   Assistant Manager - Accounts Payable, Pop-
                    Rite Soda, Los Angeles. Supervised 17 people;
                    processed approximately 500 invoices per day;
                    balanced daily disbursements with computer
                    printout.

    1965-1970   Billing Supervisor, Gardner Advertising, Los
                    Angeles. Supervised 5 people; billed
                    approximately 40 invoices per day; Accounts
                    Receivable and Accounts Payable.

EDUCATION

    Santa Fe High, Commercial Course, 1965

    REFERENCES SUPPLIED BY REQUEST.

MILLARD POLLOCK
1428 Cornelia
Brooklyn, NY 11227
(212) EV 4-3366

OBJECTIVE: To manage a general bookstore with large volume sales, and act as
buyer for same. Particularly interested in rare editions and current
literature.

EXPERIENCE

May 1984-   Store Manager, R. Altman Bookseller,
Present   Riverdale, New York.
Responsible for increase in sales of at least 25% since
handling of inventory and selection of items for special
sales. Present sales volume more than 20% above previous
goal.

February 1983-   Manager Trainee, R. Altman Bookseller,
May 1984   Daytona Beach, Florida. Trained in all phases of selling,
customer relations, sales presentations, etc.

May 1982-   Sales Clerk, Bainbridge Music Sales, Inc.,
February 1983   Springfield, Ohio. Sold sheet music; recommended special
pieces for chorale groups, instrumentalists.

EDUCATION

Attended University of Kansas September 1980 through June 1982.
Majored in Literature.

P.S. 68, Brooklyn - 1976-1979 - College Prep. Curriculum.

PROFESSIONAL AFFILIATIONS

Member of NBS. Certified completion of NBS/FLS Booksellers Program.

REFERENCES

Complete references will be furnished upon request.

```
Laura Sue Carter                    Home: (919) 421-1234
236 West Street                     Work: (919) 472-9200
Hendersville, NC 27208


PROFESSIONAL
  OBJECTIVE              Sports Wear Buyer

BUSINESS EXPERIENCE

  1982 to present        Sports Wear Buyer, Playtime, Inc.,
                         Waring, NC
                         Complete charge of women's sportswear
                         department, responsible for $300,000
                         budget; supervise staff of 6 junior
                         buyers; check, authorize payment on
                         all invoices.

  1977 to 1982           Assistant Buyer, Kronfeld's,
                         Hendersville, NC
                         Responsible for checking and
                         verifying the merchandise; coded tags
                         and records; handled all secretarial
                         duties.

  EDUCATION              B.A. 1977, Wake forest, Fine Arts

  REFERENCES             Will be furnished on request
```

David Hershfield
166 Elm Street
Framingham, MA 02189
(617) 421-6822

Objective
To secure a position for the summer of 1989 as an athletic or senior counselor. Full Red Cross training and qualifications.

Experience

Summer 1988
Athletic Counselor, Camp Wee-ta-kee, Geneva, N.Y., Responsible for all sports for the 14- to 16-year-old age group; sports included swimming, tennis, archery and riding; supervised junior counselors.

Summer 1987
Waterfront Counselor, Camp Endicott, Turham, N.H., Supervised all lake sports, including canoeing, sailing, swimming, and water skiing.

Counselor, Camp Endicott, summer of 1986. Responsible for 65 boys; instructor in basketball.

Education
Junior at University of Pennsylvania, 1989.

References
References on request.

ROBERTA CALDWELL
35 Lyndon Way
Cromwell, New Jersey 07841

201-991-0328

OBJECTIVE: To be employed as cashier in large retail store
in shopping center, preferably in Cromwell vicinity.

EXPERIENCE

1979-   <u>Cashier</u>, part-time, Bergen Supermarket, Bergen, N.J.
1989   Worked 20 hours a week as cashier at checkout counter.

1970-   <u>Assistant Bookkeeper and Cashier</u>, Howard's Retail Store.
1979   Collected and recorded mail-order payments as well as
those made in person at credit office; prepared monthly
statement; assisted bookkeeper in all record-keeping.

1965-   <u>Accounts Receivable Clerk</u>, Homowak Mart, New Bergen, N.J.
1970   Received payments made in credit office and by mail,
recorded cash, issued receipts. Prepared monthly statements to customers.

EDUCATION

1965   Completed six months' course in Business Machines at
Cromwell Business School.

1961-   Attended Cromwell High School. Completed requirements
1965   for Commercial Diploma.

REFERENCES

Furnished upon request.

Robert S. Showalter
135 Maine Avenue
Flushing, New York 11353
(212) 533-6857

SUMMARY:

Circulation management executive. Consumer, trade, business
publishing fields. Total expertise in all circulation areas,
including subscription promotion, direct response, graphics
buying, agency sales, newsstand sales, fulfillment,
computerized systems, budgets, audit requirements.

EMPLOYMENT:

Mailis Publishing Co., Inc., New York, New York. (9/87-
present)
Circulation director and member of management planning
board. Responsible for the development and implementation of
all circulation and related programs. Initiated and
implemented merchandise marketing program.

Reader's Digest, Inc., Mount Kisco, New York. (1/84-8/87)
Assistant to vice president and circulation director.
Involvement included all circulation areas, subscription
promotion, direct response programs, agency sales,
fulfillment, budgets.

Food Packaging, Inc., New York, New York. (2/82-12/83)
Assistant to vice president and circulation director.
Responsibilities included all circulation areas,
subscription promotion, direct response programs, agency
sales, newsstand, fulfillment, budget.

Computer/Data, Inc., New York, New York. (6/75-1/82)
Operations manager for computerized magazine, book, direct
mail, merchandise fulfillment and related services.

EDUCATION:

Queens College, Flushing, New York (1971-1975)
Hunter College's School of Advanced Business Administration
(1970-1971)

REFERENCES:

Available on request.

Raymond J. Stetson

99 Perry Street
New York, New York 10014

212-924-8813 (home)
212-879-5500 (business)

Professional Experience:

1983-present
Clerk, The Metropolitan Museum of Art, New York, New York
10028. Knowledge of all aspects in production and
composition of internal museum publications.
Responsibilities include photography, reduction, layout,
sizing, and printing.

1982-1983
Clerk and Assistant Bookkeeper, Basic Books Co., New York,
New York 10022. Dealings in royalty allotments to
educational publications' authors, including company as well
as author dividends. Also development of a computerization
layout and feed-in to replace manual computations.

1980-1982
Intermediate Clerk, First Jersey National Bank, Jersey City,
New Jersey 07302. Solely responsible for computer feed-in of
dealer commissions for mutual funds corporations. Control
check of stock books and balancing.

1975-1976
Clerk, First Jersey National Bank, Jersey City, New Jersey
07302. Accounts researcher, stock issuance, control of
accounts receivable for mutual funds corporations. Daily use
of telephone for communication of services to nationwide
investors and their representatives.

Educational Background:

   City College of NY, NYC 1975

References: Available on request.

EVELYN PLUMER
259 Ridge Lane
Danbury, Connecticut 06810
203-742-3301

<u>JOB</u> <u>OBJECTIVE</u>: To provide top-quality, con-
scientious service as typist and office clerk
to industrial firm in New York City.

EXPERIENCE

1985-   <u>Typist, File Clerk</u>, Feinberg Associates, Danbury,
Date   Connecticut. Assemble data from legal reports,
           type revisions and legal contracts; serve as
           relief receptionist, maintain files, and provide
           general office assistance.

1983-   <u>Typist-Receptionist</u>, Manzo Realtors, Forest Hills,
1985   New York. Served as receptionist to large Real
           Estate company; typed documents related to sale
           and purchase of property; filed records of clients
           and construction companies; maintained appointment
           schedules.

EDUCATION

Graduated with Commercial Diploma from Danbury High School,
June, 1985.

OFFICE SKILLS

Typing - 75 wpm; Shorthand - 100 wpm; Filing; Calculators;
Dictaphone; Duplicating Machines; Call Directors.

REFERENCES

Will be provided upon request

Chiala Dakazarom
465 West End Avenue
New York, New York 10023
(212) 622-4802

OBJECTIVE   Full-time employment as clerk-typist or typist-
                 receptionist in New York firm.

EXPERIENCE

June 1984-   Clerk-typist, Jorgensen International, Carteret,
present   N.J. Type data on office forms, file records,
                 provide general office assistance.

EDUCATION

1982-1984   Attended Water Valley Junior College in Buffalo,
                 N.Y. Earned A.A. in English Composition,
                 May, 1984.

OFFICE SKILLS

Typing - 50 wpm
Filing

REFERENCES

Will be provided upon request.

DAVID STEIN
31 Oak Road
Sedona, Arizona 24156
(918) 883-4156

EDUCATION
Union College, Poughkeepsie, NY
Graduated June 1988
Courses included: Marketing Research,
Financial Management, Production Management,
Introduction to Computer Systems, Accounting
I and II.

EXPERIENCE

Summers 1985-88
Allen Majors Building, Inc., Rockville
Centre, NY. Participated in inventory
control, receiving and shipping, deliveries,
advancing to counterperson.

Summers 1980-84
Jordan Lobster Farms, Inc., and North Shore
Lobster Seafood Co., Island Park, NY, and
Great Neck, NY. Responsible for preparation
of lobsters, sales, receiving and shipping,
and general maintenance.

Summers
  Part-time
  1987-88
Basic Needs, Inc.
Assisted in the running of summer curb
painting operation for various villages of
Long Island.

ACTIVITIES
Member Union College Varsity Hockey 1984-88
Participated in nationally recognized Marist
College Institute for Public Opinion, Big
Brother/Big Sister Program, Poughkeepsie, NY,
1985
Intramural Sports Program 1984-88

REFERENCES
Furnished upon request

PAUL RAYSON

(Confidential)

519 S. 4th Street
Edinburg, Texas 78539
Phone: Home: (512) 383-6655
Office: (512) 381-2515

OBJECTIVE

ADMINISTRATIVE STAFF

Research — Communication and Publications — Program Planning — Training

EXPERIENCE

1981 - present. **Assistant Professor** in Department of History, **Pan American University,**
Edinburg, Texas.
Conduct classroom lectures, discussions, examinations; lead and coordinate seminars.
Perform course design, involving research and organization. Serve on various committees—e.g., honors council and self-study committee for University reaccreditation—
entailing research and writing activity. Handle diverse adminis-trative duties, including
coordination of interdepartmental honors program, supervision of research projects,
student counseling and recruitment.

Efforts have been instrumental in upgrading awareness of students in areas pertinent to
fields of study; in attracting new students to school and department; and in improving
personal skills in communication. Among accomplishments: Through course organization, coordinated library of visuals, and revised and modernized reading list, succeeded in
revitalizing two honors courses that had suffered severe enrollment losses under predeces-
sor. Through extensive independent research, formulated and implemented pioneering
courses that have earned high standing among departmental offerings.

1978-1981. **Assistant Professor** at **Falls View College,** Falls View, Mississippi; following
brief fill-in assignment during emergency situation at West Chester College, West Chester, Pennsylvania. Performed teaching, research, administrative and other functions
similar to those above.
Previously, **Graduate & Undergraduate Student;** with concurrent employment (1976-
1978) as **Library Technician** in information services for **Free Library of New York,** and
as **Music Director** for church.

EDUCATION / PROFESSIONAL QUALIFICATIONS / LANGUAGES

Ph.D. and A.M. degrees in American Civilization, from University of Pennsylvania,
Philadelphia. Recipient of Woodrow Wilson, University and Harrison Fellowships, 1978.

(Continued)

Paul Rayson -2

B.A. (with honors) in American Studies, State University of New York at Buffalo. Elected to Phi Beta Kappa.

Publications: Author of Essay "Containing Communism: the Art of Getting Along," in Reason; and of book reviews in American Quarterly.

Languages: Essential fluency in French; also some Spanish.

REFERENCES Will be furnished on request.

REBECCA CARTER
14 Gray Place
New Hyde Park, NY 11545
(516) 921-8950
(516) 815-2600

OBJECTIVE: Obtain a career-oriented position providing opportunties for advancement while allowing me to utilize my experience and specialized work skills.

EDUCATION: **Cornell College**
B.S. in Business: 5/87
Double Major: Finance and Computer Information Systems.
Cumulative GPA 3.6 on a 4.0 scale.

ACADEMIC HONORS: National Presidential Scholarship
Member Delta Mu Delta Honor Society
Member Cornell College Wall Street Careers Seminar
Dean's List First Honors
Cornell College Scholarship

COMPUTER SKILLS:
Hardware IBM PC/PC-XT/PC-AT, IBM 3270, IBM 3081 with VM 370, IBM 4381, VAX II/780, PDP 1170, IBM 6670 Printer, IBM 3289 Line Printer

Software MMS, APGS, IPG, APL, Lotus 1-2-3, D-Base III, Diagram Master, Framework, Chartmaster, Signmaster, Writing Assistant, Graphwriter, LINDO, IFPS, Basic, COBOL

WORK EXPERIENCE:

6/87 - Present **H.R. Hutton & Co., Inc.,** New York, NY
- Account Administrator within the Custodian Services Department of Broadcort Capital Corporation.
- Liaison between Merrill Lynch and its customers ensuring that specialized and individualized service is rendered to customers.
- Achieve settlement of all trades on a timely basis through the use of journal entries, receive/deliver instructions and trade affirmations.
- Monitor and review margin and cash accounts for proper entries.
- Responsible for investing all customers' cash balances into any of numerous interest

(Continued)

143

              bearing vehicles.
- Report to customers daily on status of accounts and activities within accounts such as receives, delivers, tender offers and DK's.
- Maintain accurate bookkeeping records to satisfy customer inquiries, as well as internal audits.

9/86 - 5/87   **ITT - Information Systems Group Headquarters,** Long Beach, NY
- Data Analyst in the Product Planning Evaluations Department responsible for tracking monthly product sales data by division, calculating deviations from proposed annual plan and interpreting the division's success in attaining the plan.

REFERENCES: Furnished upon request.

David Morise
121 Wayne Place
Bronxville, NY 12614
(914) 821-4463

EDUCATION

May 1984

Fontbonne College
B.A., Mathematics - GPA: 3.94/4.0

In addition to the study of theoretical and applied mathematics, concentration has been in the areas of computer science and business. Courses include FORTRAN, BASIC, COBOL, Systems Science, Operations Research, Accounting, Economics and Investments.

EXPERIENCE

September 1981
to Present

Atlas Corporation
Larchmont, New York 10538

SCIENTIFIC PROGRAMMER/DATA BASE ANALYST
(Full Time May 1983 to August 1983 (CO-OP) -
Part Time 25-35 hours per week, August 1983 to Present)

Assigned to the Computer Aided Technology Project in the Scientific Data Base Management Systems group. Duties and responsibilities include:
- Participation in efficiency testing of Model 204 Data Base Management System to be used in the Computer Aided Design Drafting system.
- Participation in the design of Back-Up and Recovery techniques and Security Features of the system.
- Design and initialization of Data Bases.
- Application User Support for Model 204 system.
- Teaching Data Base classes.

Application Programming was done in FORTRAN using TSO on IBM 3033 MVS JES III systems.

(Same Organization)
SCIENTIFIC PROGRAMMER
(Full Time (CO-OP) - January 1983 to May 1983
                     - May 1982 to December 1982
                     - September 1981 to December 1981)

Duties and responsibilities included:
- Tape Management for Flight Simulation Labs.
- Graphical Analysis of simulated flight data.
- Programming in FORTRAN, MATLOC, and CSMP to analyze a digital control system for aircraft.
- Development of modeling programs to simulate the effectiveness of the control system on the aircraft.

REFERENCE SENT ON REQUEST

HARRIET BACH
22 Windover Road
White Plains, NY 12148
(914) 948-7190

OBJECTIVE

A financial control or analysis position with management growth potential where knowledge of computers and finance can be combined.

EXPERIENCE

Security National Bank, White Plains, NY

1984 to 1989
-**Controller,** Shareholder Processing product line. Accountable officer for financial control, reporting and analysis, and contract compliance associated with the divestiture of Shareholder products. a) Directed external cash exchanges of approximately $10 million annually under contractual terms. b) Budgeted for operating expenses of about $8 million annually. c) Problem resolution/negotiation with buyer's Controller. d) Supervised staff of four.

1981 to 1983
Promoted four times from Staff Assistant to Controller while assigned to various Corporate Trust product lines: Bearer Bonds, Mortgage Backed Securities, and Information Services. Developed monthly product profitability and expense reports. Investigated expenses, allocated charges and business issues impacting product costs. Capital budgets for projects up to $20 million.

Sears, Inc. International Headquarters, White Plains, NY

1980
-**Systems Analyst Trainee.** Trained to write computer programs in structured COBOL, code own JCL, debug programs with Pro-test, use TSO and Pan-Velet, on an IBM 370.

Ohio State University, Columbus, Ohio

1975 to 1978
-**Administrative Assistant, Clinical Science Program,** College of Human Medicine. Managed staff support for six on-campus courses and one statewide clerkship. a) designed and implemented complex schedules for interviews, physical examinations, etc. b) secured physical facilities, hospital support, and equipment; c) supervised

(Continued)

              clerical and other employees.

1975   **-Administrative Assistant for Undergraduate Education,** Sociology Department. Found and recommended professors to teach extension courses. Academically advised undergraduates.

1969 to   **-Teaching Assistant,** Sociology Department. Half
  1974   time teaching or administrative positions for various faculty.

except
1970 to   **-Clerk,** Libraries. Supervised student employees;
  1972   maintained Reserve Room journal articles.

EDUCATION

              M.B.A. 1980. Finance. Ohio State University.
              M.A. 1976. Sociology.
              B.A. 1969. Sociology.

REFERENCES: Available upon request.

SUSAN EMORY
118 W. 79th St.
N.Y.C., NY 10023

Home (212) 815-2324   Office (212) 718-3200

SUMMARY OF EXPERIENCE

Diversified accounting/auditing and management experience. Extensive background in financial analysis and accounting systems and controls. Currently as a working Controller responsible for timely financial reports.

6/77-Present   **David King Co., Inc., NY**

Controller: Managing the financial, accounting and data processing functions. Supervising the maintenance of books and records, and the office staff. In charge of preparation of financial projections, budgets, analysis, statements and tax reports. Advising management on opportunities and on actions to improve profitability.

6/71-5/77   **Paris Furniture Co., NY**

Accountant, Asst. Controller: Responsible for the maintenance of company general ledger, preparation of financial reports, cash receivables and inventory control.

6/63-5/71   **A. R. Sykes & Co., Harrison, NY**

Senior Accountant: Supervised staff of seven accountants whose major tasks were the design and implementation of new integrated accounting systems for new and existing divisions and branches of the company. Conducted and performed field auditing, financial and operational.

9/62-5/63   **Otis Elevator Co., Yonkers, NY**

Accountant: Performed diversified audit assignments.

EDUCATION   Fordham University, 1962, B.B.A. Major: Accounting

Fordham University, 1969, Post Graduate Degree

L.I.U., New York Master Degree Courses:
Financial statements, analysis, quantitative analysis, and quantitative analysis for business research 1974

Accounting Qualifying Certificate, State of New York, 1983

CPA Candidate

LANGUAGES   Fluent in Arabic Language

REFERENCES   Furnished upon request

Samuel J. Taylor
300 Riverside Drive
New York, New York 10025

212-797-3149

RESUME CAPSULE:

Four years' experience as copywriter for leading
publisher, as well as free-lance writing of film
reviews over the past five years.

EXPERIENCE:

May 1982–
Present

<u>Copywriter</u>, Curtis-Hall, Inc., Publishers, Bergen-
ville, New Jersey. Create and write advertising
for direct-mail for premium sales and professional
books; do layouts, designs and paste-ups for cover
material; train new copywriters; condense copy
from full-size publications into "mini" books for
premium sales.

September 1981–
Present

<u>Free-lance Film Reviewer</u>, for various news media.
Write reviews on educational films for radio and
newspaper presentation.

EDUCATION:

M.F.A., June 1981, New York University
B.A., June 1979, Cornell University

SPECIAL HONORS

Phi Beta Kappa
Smithsonia Scholarship Award - 1977 and 1978.

REFERENCES

Will be furnished upon request.

COPYWRITER (SENIOR)/ADMINISTRATOR

CHRISTINA KAYE
40 Kalmbach Road
New City, New York   10956
(914) 222-3596

RESUME CAPSULE: Four years' experience as Copy Chief for leading sales
                   agency, two years as Copy Chief and Senior Copywriter
                   as well as several years of free-lance work for major
                   producers of cosmetics, athletic organizations and
                   advertising firms.

EXPERIENCE

October 1979–   **Copy Chief**, Martin Bruckner Agency, New York City.
April 1989   In charge of selection, execution and all presentation
                     of promotional sales material, for all accounts
                     including leading cosmetic, lingerie, knitted garments,
                     and linen manufacturers.

May 1978–   **Senior Copywriter**, Panels Unlimited, New York City.
September 1979   Sales promotion ads and literature to trade, consumer
                     ads, and industrial copy.

June 1976–   **Assistant Copy Chief**, Allied Radio, New York City.
April 1978   Sales promotion, direct mail, trade and catalog copy,
                     consumer ads for all departments. Responsible for
                     special cooperative advertising with producers such
                     as Goldenrod Ceramics, Cornucopia Stoneware and Devon
                     Cosmetics.

September 1974–   **Copy/Marketing Trainee**, McCabe Advertising, Inc., New
May 1976   York City. Received training in all phases of copywriting/
                     marketing.

EDUCATION

B.B.A., June 1974, Pace Institute.

Graduate Work in Sociology, Advanced School of Social Research, Staten Island,
New York, September 1972–1974.

Executive Training Program, McCabe Advertising, September 1974–May 1976.

REFERENCES

Will be furnished upon request.

MALCOLM LIDDY
290 West 11th Street
New York, New York 10014
212-243-5022

BUSINESS EXPERIENCE

1978-present   Credit Manager, Bonanza Adhesives, Inc., Milwau-
                     kee, Wisconsin. One of the nation's largest
                     producers of adhesive-backed products (labels,
                     tapes, etc.). Established all credit and collec-
                     tion systems, developed accounts receivable and
                     collections systems. Conducted credit analysis,
                     followed up all collections. Managed credit and
                     collection staff, personally reviewed all major
                     accounts and adjusted ratings. Periodically
                     reviewed and improved upon collections procedures.

1974-1978   Credit Accountant, North American Bank, N.Y.
                     Served as assistant to loan review supervisor.
                     All phases of credit appraisal, discounting of
                     commercial papers, handling of insolvencies.

EDUCATION

B.S. - 1974 - New York University. Majored in accounting and
business law, with minor in banking and finance.

REFERENCES

Will be furnished upon request.

Jerry Korban
345 Brighton Avenue
West New York, New Jersey 07093
Telephone: (201) 965-9845

Work Experience: Hazen and Sawyer, Engineers
360 Lexington Avenue
New York, New York 10017 (212) 986-0033

Work performed: trusted to solve unique problems throughout
firm. Developed and negotiated with vendors of furniture,
instruments (cameras, calculators, overhead projectors, etc.),
stationery, and local and long-distance messenger services;
supervised in-house mailroom and duplicating services. Designed covers; dealt with typographers, printers, and word
processing suppliers; supervised production of reports and proposals. Responsible for office maintenance; dealt with building
maintenance crew and outside firms; organized work parties for
files reduction program; organized filing system; controlled 1100
drawings for a $43,000,000 project. Handled interviews for
clerical staff; organized parties and seminars; performed library
and media research as required.
November 1984 to present

Raventos International Corporation
150 Fifth Avenue
New York, New York 10011 (212) 924-2490

Work performed: marketed an architectural service that reno-
vated, designed and constructed church buildings; did writing
and layout of brochures; wrote research reports on current developments in liturgy and architecture.
June 1982 to September 1984

Fort Worth Community Theatre
Fort Worth, Texas

Work performed: acting, stage managing, set building, lights,
sound and publicity.
September 1981 to May 1982

Education: Currently enrolled in Master of Urban Planning program at
NYU.

State University of New York at Stony Brook
Stony Brook, New York
B.A. English
Graduated: 1980

ROSETTA DEL'ORIFICE
2109 Broadway
New York, New York 10023
212-787-3200

JOB OBJECTIVE: Position with food processor as staff
                  specialist.

EXPERIENCE

1985-present   Assistant Dietitian (part-time), Food Services
                Department, Masonic Temple, Detroit, Michigan.
                Helped plan menus and supervised preparation of
                all meals.

Summers   Assistant to Chief Dietitian, Marlboro State
1981-1985   Hospital, Marlboro, Michigan. Helped translate
                convalescent diets into actual meals, selected
                and delivered special meals to diet patients.

EDUCATION

B.S. degree, Michigan State University 1985. Nutrition major.
Graduate courses on Environmental Effect on Man and His Menu,
Special Food for the Elderly, and Food Chemistry.

These courses provided an excellent background in elements of
nutrition as related to ecology, problems of the elderly, and
commercial food processing.

HONORS

Dean's List throughout four years of college.

REFERENCES

Will be furnished upon request.

Brian Mitchell
26 Court Street
San Francisco, California 94165
(415) 822-5621

Objective: To continue a career as a Medical Director in a
large corporation; seeking to relocate in the
southeast.

<u>Experience:</u>

1980-
present   **Medical Director,** Acem Elevator Co., San
Francisco, California.
Supervise all medical activities and am
responsible for staff of three doctors, twelve
nurses, three lab technicians and two secretaries.
Supervise entire medical program: physical
examinations, blood tests, medical emergencies,
administration of flu school programs. Set up
employee health plans. Liaison with insurance
companies and Workmen's Compensation.

1961-1970   **Physician,** Hill & Hill, Inc., Los Angeles,
California.
Conducted physical examinations, treated injuries,
handled medical emergencies. Administered
Workmen's Compensation.

<u>Education:</u>

1960   Internship -- Ithaca Hospital, Ithaca, New York.

1959   Doctor of Medicine, Cornell Medical School,
Ithaca, New York.

1949   B.S. -- Cornell University, Ithaca, New York.

<u>References</u> <u>on</u> <u>request.</u>

ALBERTO ROSSI
One Top Stone Drive
Toledo, Ohio 43614
(419) 361-7444

OBJECTIVE

To serve as draftsman in supervisory capacity with manufacturer of mechanical or electrical products.

EXPERIENCE

1984–present
Supervisory Draftsman, Toledo Castings, Inc., Toledo, Ohio. Implement engineering designs of pipes and fittings into working plans. Work with both synthetic fibre and cast iron pipes and fittings. Examine and give recommendations on cost, durability, and feasibility of production designs.

1979–1984
Senior Draftsman, Fire Engine Division, Supreme Truck Manufacturers, Romulus, NY. Assisted Senior Draftsmen in designing basic parts of mountings placed on truck chassis in constructing fire engines. Position provided invaluable training in gross and detailed design and firsthand work with engineers and craftsmen.

EDUCATION

Certificate in Mechanical Drafting, Greenfield Trade School, Greenfield, New York—1979

REFERENCES

Will be furnished upon request.

NAME: Thomas Wolfson

BUSINESS ADDRESS AND TELEPHONE NUMBER: Coolidge Institution on War, Revolution and Peace, Stanford University, Stanford, California 94305; 617-734-2979

HOME ADDRESS: 209 Southside Street, Springton, California 90916

FIELDS OF STUDY: <u>History</u>   <u>Political Science</u> (outside field)
                  Russia since 1500 (major)   Soviet Foreign Policy
                  Eastern Europe since 1453   International Communism
                  Western Europe since 1789   Marxist Theory

FOREIGN LANGUAGES: Russian (active knowledge)
                    French (active knowledge)
                    German (passive knowledge)

FELLOWSHIPS: Teaching Assistantship, Indiana University, 1978-79, 1979-80
              Graduate Assistantship, Indiana University, 1980-81, 1981-82
              Doctoral Student Grant-in-Aid for Research, Indiana University, 1982-83

DISSERTATION: Rebuilding the Russian Army, 1909-14: A Study in the Formation of Policy under Nicholas II

CURRENT POSITION: Information Editor, Hoover Institution, 1979-present.

RESPONSIBILITIES OF CURRENT POSITION: Primary responsibilities are those of Assistant Editor of the <u>Russian Review</u>, a scholarly journal sponsored by the Hoover Institution. Read and evaluate incoming manuscripts, edit accepted manuscripts (both for content and for style), correspond with authors, undertake basic bibliographic research related to accepted manuscripts, proofread at all stages of publication, assign new books to reviewers in appropriate fields, and secure necessary copyrights.

CAREER GOALS: Would like to work with a press interested in publishing scholarly books. Feel my broad liberal arts background provides a good frame of reference for reading and evaluating manuscripts submitted for publication. Having learned the basics of editing on the staff of a specialized quarterly, now desire to move to a position with broader scope and more potential for development and advancement.

EDUCATION: Ph.D. (major: history), 1989 (expected), Indiana University
            M.A. (major: history), 1979, Indiana University, Bloomington, Indiana
            A.B. (major: history), 1977, Duke University, Durham, North Carolina

REFERENCES: On request.

Gilbert G. Crossens
482 East 46th Street
New York, New York 10017

212-462-0934

OBJECTIVE   To apply background and interest in History to
             editing educational books on Early American History.

EXPERIENCE

1983-1989   Instructor, Montveil Seminary, Montveil,
             Pennsylvania. Principles of Economics, Early
             American History, History of Economic Thought.

1981-1982   Instructor, St. Agnes Convent, Convent Station,
             N.J. Comparative Economic Systems, U.S.
             Government, U.S. History.

1980-1981   Instructor, Midvale College, Brooklyn. Economic
             Institutions, American History.

1979-1980   Editor, The World Today, Historical Society of
             Philadelphia. Edited encyclopedia commentaries
             on current events, particularly related to
             American Politics and Historical Events.

EDUCATION
  Ph.D., Economics, Pennsylvania State University - 1984
  M.A., History, Pennsylvania State University - 1978
  B.A., Economics/History, Fordham College, New Jersey - 1975

REFERENCES
  Available on request.

JOHN W. BOSITINO
2109 Broadway
New York, New York 10023
212 SU 7-2200

OBJECTIVE: To obtain position as Senior Editor with publisher of high school/college texts, general trade.

EXPERIENCE

11/79 -
present

Editor, Brace Publishing Corporation, New York, NY. Assisted the editorial director in reviewing and selecting general trade and business education titles, establishing publishing priorities, scheduling. Extensive author guidance in developing and refining manuscripts. Supervised freelance design and editing. Some basic book design.

2/76-11/79

Senior Editing Supervisor, Pitt Division, Hill-Grenier Book Company, New York, NY. Manuscript review, editing, production control to bound books. Feature writing, revisions. Thorough training in layout and design.

6/75-2/76

Production Editor, Glen Publishing Company, Knoxville, Pennsylvania. All foreign language books, both hardbound and paperback. Supervision of freelance and in-house copyediting. Close work with authors, artists, designers. At least twenty-five titles per year.

7/72-9/74

Staff Editor, Alan Wilson & Sons, Inc., New York, NY. Copyediting in civil and electrical engineering, mathematics, biology, physics, economics, programming.

EDUCATION

M.A., English Literature/Linguistics, June, 1979, New York University, Graduate School of Arts and Sciences.

B.A. (Majors in English and Spanish), June 1968, Winchester College, Milton, New York.

REFERENCES

Will be furnished upon request.

Dennis Wong
256 Hill Street
San Francisco, California 94165
Phone 415 324-8461

Experience:

5/78 - present	**Apex Telephone, Inc., San Francisco, CA**

Senior Marketing Engineer for both active and passive electronic components. Serviced Australian government and original equipment manufacturers.

1/70 - 3/78	**Spero Missiles, Carmen, CA**

Senior Systems Integration Engineer, responsible for the complete integration of the "Black Box" electrical sub-system of the Polaris Missile into the entire weapon system utilizing coordination drawings.

8/62 - 11/69	**Northeast Telephone Laboratories, New York, NY**

Member of the Technical Staff responsible for the analysis of both wire-spring and reed-spring relays as well as mechanical switches. Assistant Project Engineer on the development of electronic telephone equipment: e.g., push-button dialing, direct distance dialing, and solid-state ringers.

Education:

1962   MIT, B.S. in Electrical Engineering

References:

Available upon request

MARK BERGER
15 OVERLOOK DRIVE
CLIFTON, NEW JERSEY 07815
(201) 776-4232

PROFESSIONAL EXPERIENCE:

March 1984-present

CARNEY, INC., CLIFTON, NEW JERSEY
Manager of Logistics at the Corporate Transportation/
Physical Distribution Division. Responsibilities
include systems analysis, logistic planning, facilities design, development and implementation of major
improvement projects; specialize in the areas of
cost reduction and analytical statistics.

February 1983-February
1984

AGAR ALUMINUM, TEL AVIV, ISRAEL
Project Engineer. Responsibilities include
production control, methods, cost benefit analysis, and supervision of projects through all
phases of production.

January 1982-February
1983

BARKER'S INSTRUMENTS, INC., NYACK, NEW YORK
Apprenticeship program specializing in production
of high precision components for the aerospace
industry utilizing computerized Numerical Control
equipment.

EDUCATION:

NEW YORK UNIVERSITY, NEW YORK, NEW YORK
M.S. in Industrial Engineering and Operation
Research, 1983

"TECHNION" - Tel Aviv Institute of Technology
B.S. in Industrial Engineering and Computer
Science, 1980

SPECIALTIES:

Computer Science and Operation Research with respect
to production planning, systems analysis, system design
and management controls, using computer applications
and simulation techniques.

OBJECTIVES:

To engage in an established and highly sophisticated
Engineering/Management Department where there is an
opportunity for potential development and growth.

References on request.

BEVERLY STANLEY
200 East 15th St.
Philadelphia, PA 18415
(215) 775-7372
(212) 779-8900

SKILLS

Versatile professional seeks responsible, diversified position in fast-paced environment. Extensive experience as generalist in both business and academic worlds. Specializations: writing, research, editing, systems organization, problem solving, project supervision and coordination, staff training. All office functions including Xerox 860 word processing.

EDUCATION

Skidmore College, B.A. with Honors
Union College, M.A.

EMPLOYMENT

1983-present

Executive Assistant to the Dean of the Arts
The City College of The City University of Philadelphia
Manage office, develop and implement office systems and procedures, supervise secretarial aides, draft grant proposals, coordinate communications between university offices, external organizations and community groups; student advisement; special projects.

1982-83

Adjunct Instructor, University of Pennsylvania
Taught Business English/Administrative Writing to working adults.

1982

Executive Assistant to Vice President-in-Charge
Telecommunications Division, Manufacturers Hanover Trust
Managed office; right hand to CEO. Coordinated move of Telecommunications Division to new quarters. Time limited project.

1977-82

Free-Lance Administrative Assistant, Writer, Photographer
Performed administrative and secretarial tasks for large corporations, small businesses and educational organizations. Many assignments for top management (e.g., V.P.-in-charge, Private Banking, Citibank; Director of Publications, Arthur Young & Co.; Director Expository Writing, New York University.) Photographic work published (magazines; book/record covers; museum catalog). Broad range of writing, editing and research assignments (e.g., market research, Interior Design Magazine; lecture series, Big Apple Circus; audio-visual programs, CBS Labs, Olympic Media Information; manuscript copy-editing, Behavioral Publications).

1976

Public Relations Associate
Hurley & Hurley, Inc.
Introduced services of lighting designer to architects, city planners. High-level telephone sales. Free-lance.

(Continued)

Beverly Stanley -2

1973-74 <u>Administrative Assistant</u>
Media International School
Coordinated office functions for elementary school; liaison with administrators, teachers, children, parents, United Nations personnel.

1969-72 <u>Research Associate</u>
Designed questionnaires, conducted interviews, evaluated data, wrote final report to client for educational consulting firm. Managed office and assisted in research projects for physician/scientist.

References upon request

KAREN GAINES
10 Warburton Ave.
Yonkers, NY 10701
(914) 963-4434
(914) 948-2800

Experience:

Executive Secretary   January 88-present
Miller & Kaplen, Inc.

Assistant to the executive vice president and director, the group
manager, and the supervisor of the healthcare division.
Responsibilities include assisting in planning of special events,
seminars and press conferences, preparation of monthly client
billing, coordinating client meetings and travel arrangements,
daily communication with clients, vendors, and general office
duties.

Account Coordinator   August 86-January 88
Famous Agents, Inc.

Assistant to executive vice president in charge of international
entertainment marketing. Coordinated media & celebrity
participation in special events, prepared monthly client billing,
monthly operations report, designed new business presentation,
researched new business opportunities, planned all client
meetings, travel, and general office duties.

Group Secretary   January 85-August 86

Worked with senior vice president and vice president.
Responsibilities included planning of client meetings, travel
arrangements, monthly activities report, forecast of time
charges, supervision of six secretaries and general office
duties.

Secretary   January 84-January 85

Worked with a vice president and three account executives.
Responsibilities included typing, client contact, internal
correspondence, meeting and travel arrangements.

Business Office Representative   January 81-January 84
Bell Laboratories, Inc., Nassau, NY

Coordinated new business and telephone repair orders in Nassau
County.

Education:

Fashion Institute of Technology
New York, NY, 1981

Currently studying Fashion Design.

References: Available upon request.

LORRAINE HOFFMAN
56-26 121st Street
Cambria Heights, New York 11411   Telephone: (212) 693-3369

BUSINESS EXPERIENCE

September 1978-present

Executive Secretary to Research Director, Carter Baron Research Center, New York, NY. Handle personal and business correspondence, business records; make travel arrangements, maintain travel schedules; prepare and edit technical literature, catalogs, promotional brochures; arrange for placement of advertisements and notices in scientific journals; assist in the design and construction of several traveling displays for educational seminars and conventions on annual basis; attend these seminars to assist in promotional programs and presentations.

February 1977-August 1978

Executive Secretary, Baker Johnson Company, Brooklyn, New York. Executive secretary to President and Vice president of this small public relations company; acted as liaison between several account managers and sales representatives of client companies; set up conferences and presentations for prospective clients; maintained schedules.

May 1974-February 1977

Dictaphone Secretary, Gibbs Importers, Queens, New York. Transcribed correspondence, bills of lading, contracts, all necessary documents involved in receiving imported merchandise for distribution to stores.

EDUCATIONAL BACKGROUND

B.A., June 1974, Columbia University, New York
Major: English Literature

REFERENCES

Will be furnished upon request

Mario Pesiri
859 Hobart Street
San Francisco, California 94110
(415) 875-0922

Objective: To secure a responsible position in Financial
                Management with potential for challenge and
                fulfillment.

Education:

1984-1986   **Stanford University**, Stanford, California
                Graduate School of Business Administration
                September 1986--Currently enrolled in second year
                electives in finance. President and founder of the
                Stanford Finance Club. Member of the Committee on
                Placement Services.

1980-1984   **Stanford University**
                Degree: B.A.--Cum Laude, Political Science,
                Economics
                January 1984--Elected to Pi Sigma Alpha (Political
                Science Honor Society) and participated in
                intercollegiate athletics (Co-captain, Varsity
                Wrestling)

Experience:

9/85-present   **Kidder, Peabody and Co., Inc.**, San Francisco,
                California
                Intern--Internship in Financial Accounting and
                Treasury. Activities participated in are standard
                accounting, budgeting process, variance analysis,
                credit approval, management of bank balances and
                short-term money management. Furthermore, while in
                Treasury participated in activities related to
                city's tender offer.

9/84-9/85   **United California Bank**, San Francisco, California
                Administrative Trainee assigned to Commercial
                Loan.
                Responsibilities were to provide financial data to
                Commercial Account Officers, control and correct
                accounts held within the Automated Financial
                System. Principal accomplishments were the
                institution of procedures and controls, with
                respect to United California's Education
                Assistance Program, and the collection of arrears.

                Summer and part-time employment with: San
                Francisco Public Library, St. Peter's Hospital,
                Woolworth and Company, and El Rancho.

References: Furnished upon request.

Kevin M. Burk
412 Fernwood Street
Floral Park, New York 11047
(212) FL7-9872

Objective: To obtain a challenging position in the area of finance.

Education: Saint John's University, Jamaica, New York
Graduate School of Business Administration
Degree: M.B.A., August 1989
Concentration: Finance
Grade Average: 3.3 (4=A)

Manhattan College, Riverdale, New York
Degree: B.S., 1988
Double Major: Economics and Biology

Experience: Four Corners Inn, Glen Oaks, New York
Cook and bartender; presently a 15-hour week.

1/88-10/88   Fischer's Motors, New Hyde Park, New York
Worked under the controller in improving the inventory
system.

7/87-12/87   Pinewood Bar and Grill, Riverdale, New York
Bartender.

Summer 1986   Cohen's Transport Service, Bronx, New York
Delivered U.S. mail to post offices from a distribution
center before classes.

Summer 1985   Penn Central Railroad, New York, New York
Crossing watchman and track gang.

Summer 1984   Nuzzi Contractors, Floral Park, New York
Truck and container maintenance.

Extracurricular   Resident Advisor; Varsity Soccer Captain; Fraternity Social
Activities: Chairman; Initiator of College Spring Soccer Program; Member
of Omicron Delta Kappa - national honorary.

References: Available upon request.

Jose L. Hernandez
R.D. 143
Rutherford, New Jersey   07299
(201) 966-4985

Objective: To obtain a position as Investment Analyst.

Education: **Rutherford State College**, Rutherford, New Jersey
Graduate School of Business Administration
Degree: M.B.A.
Graduated: August 1989

Seton College, Newark, New Jersey
Degree: B.A.
Graduated: May 1987
Concentration: History/Economics

Experience: **American Motor Credit Corporation**, Port Jervis, New York
7/88-5/89   Presented finance packages (equity and lease) to retail
customers of truck, farm, and construction equipment.
Trained salesman of franchised dealerships in the presentation of finance plans. Handled retail collections and
repossessions.

1/87-7/88   **Brown's Motor Acceptance Corporation**, Newark, New Jersey
Conducted wholesale audits, retail collections and
repossessions.

10/86-1/87   **Friendly Finance Corporation**, Union, New Jersey
Conducted interviews of potential customers; handled retail
collections.

7/84-9/86   **Kodak Corporation**, Hackensack, New Jersey
Chemical Operator.

3/83-6/84   **Volkswagen Parts Division**, Ramsey, New Jersey
Materials Handler.

References: Furnished upon request.

Gerald H. Stengel
24 West 65th Street
Brooklyn, New York
(212) 778-5901

EMPLOYMENT RECORD:

1981 - To Present   Manage Short-Term portfolio for Raleigh
Insurance Co. and subsidiaries, liaison with
banks and dealers. Manage New York Office.

1979-1980   Commercial Paper Salesman -   L.S. Martin and
Company

1965-1979   Commercial Paper Salesman -   D.D. Stern and
Company
Montreal

Activities included extensive dealings in
selling Commercial Paper and related money
market instruments. Negotiations involved
corporations in Canada and the United States.
In addition to supervision and maintenance of
existing markets, have a proven record for
the development and establishment of numerous
new money market instruments. Experience
facilitated a substantial knowledge of United
States and Canadian securities and financial
markets.

EDUCATION: Graduated Ohio State University, B.A., 1965.
Graduated Marietta College Business School
specializing in general business practices,
with emphasis on accounting.

POSITION OBJECTIVE: Seeks a challenging and responsible position
on the staff of a large progressive
corporation where vast experience in short-
term money market may be utilized; or seeks
affiliation with a brokerage house dealing in
activities of the money market.
Position should provide an atmosphere
conducive to professional growth and
achievement, and one where initiative will be
welcomed.

SUMMARY OF   Over 19 years of diversified practical
QUALIFICATIONS: experience dealing in the following vital
categories:

(Continued)

"Make Markets" in Commercial Paper . . .
Bankers Acceptances . . . Treasury Bills . .
. in both U.S. and Canadian markets. Offers
excellent leadership qualities combined with
ingenuity and flexibility, proven ability to
pioneer in new techniques and projects,
culminating in outstanding success.
Coordinates and communicates effectively at
all levels, and experienced in applying
principles of good management in motivating
maximum performance and efficiency among
subordinate personnel.

References available on request.

CLAUDIA ROGERS
16 Bryant Park
Scarsdale, NY 12465
(914) 968-4822

OBJECTIVE: To secure an entry level position where my
interest in financial management can be utilized
and developed.

EDUCATION: Masters in Business Administration, with Honors
Major: Financial Management
Pace University
White Plains, New York
1989

Bachelor of Arts
Major: Psychology
Elmira College
Elmira, New York
1987

EMPLOYMENT   Susan Marlowe Figure Salons
1987-1989   200 Hamilton Avenue
White Plains, New York
Assistant Manager/Exercise Instructor
Duties: Supervision of employees in the manager's
absence, program sales, conducting calisthenics
classes, servicing members, planning and
coordinating promotional events, completing daily
statistical reports.

1985-1987   Tompkins County Department of Social Services
108 East Green Street
Ithaca, New York
Senior Welfare Examiner
Duties: Total supervision of five welfare
examiners. Hiring, consultations, evaluations,
group and individual conferences with workers, and
interpreting state and federal regulations for
workers. Examined and authorized all paperwork and
budgets. Liaison with other social service
agencies in the community. Interviewing applicants
for public assistance, documenting all information
and determining financial eligibility.

REFERENCES: On request.

JASON PARKER LOGAN
Two Connecticut Avenue
Menlo Park, California 94025
(415) 677-8834

EXPERIENCE:

Financial Planning and Analysis

Responsible for preparation of all quarterly and annual production and financial forecasts. Designed simulation model currently used to prepare divisional macroeconomic forecasts, reducing forecasting time by 80% while improving timeliness and accuracy. Increased fourfold the number of corporate operating departments using these forecast data.

Atex Data Research, Greenwood, California. 1983-Present

Product Costing and Development

Directly responsible for preparation of all product cost forecasts. Develop corporate pricing policy and supporting economic justifications required by government regulatory agencies. Determine optimal intra-divisional allocation of resources. Improved costing techniques have significantly enhanced the competitiveness of product pricing.

Markham & Assoc., Stamford, Connecticut. 1978-1983

Statistical Analysis

Developed and maintained detailed library of divisional operating statistics. Provided senior management with monthly and year-to-date comparisons of business results and financial forecasting information.

Business Sales Inc., Bridgeport, Connecticut. 1975-1978

Marketing Planning

Tested revenue/expense impact of specific marketing strategy changes. Appointed internal marketing planning consultant to major mideast corporation (Saudia) reporting to Board of Directors.

Mideast Data Inc., Stamford, Connecticut. 1973-1975

EDUCATION: M.A., Columbia University, New York. 1977
            B.A., UCLA, Los Angeles, California. 1973

OBJECTIVE: Position in economic/business planning with a major financial institu-
            tion affording an opportunity for advancement based on achievement.

References available upon request.

ROBERT ROME
110 Gray Place
Nashville, TN 37204
(615) 787-4193

OBJECTIVE

To actively participate as a team member for improvement in the profitability and growth of a company.

PROFILE

Dependable, hard working, and self starter; possess managerial ability for problem solving, getting things done, and meeting deadlines.

EXPERIENCE

Loft & Johns, Inc. March 1982 to Present.

<u>Manager</u> - Budgeting & Planning. Primarily responsible for
* Direct coordination and assimilation of Budget Plan which includes sales forecast, operating budget, and capital expenditure plan.
* Preparation of detailed operating budgets, both annual and rollover for each strategic business unit and corresponding actual performance reports.
* Review and analyze monthly and quarterly variances and recommend corrective action to the management.
* Preparation of cashflow projections, flash and actual income statement.
* Special projects.
In addition, also responsible for retail stores accounting, cash management and payroll administration, reporting directly to the Controller; supervising four people in the Finance Department.
<u>Major</u> <u>Accomplishments</u>:
* Improved corporation's ability to utilize cash generated from retail stores through the use of online reporting system.
* Recommended to management to reorganize some of the unprofitable operations.

Tennessee Power & Light, Inc.   August 1976 to March 1982.

Manufacturer of hydraulic and other industrial valves. Sales $16 - 18 MM.
<u>Manager</u> <u>-</u> <u>Financial</u> <u>Reports</u> <u>&</u> <u>Analysis/Manager</u> <u>-</u> <u>General</u> <u>Accounting</u>.
Job Responsibilities:
* Develop, organize and prepare short and long range Profit Plan which included income and cash flow

projection and capital expenditure plan.
* Prepare capital expenditure justification request using discounted cash flow and Pay Back methods.
* Review and analyze actual results and prepare trend and variance analysis.
* Forecasting overhead rates for pricing government quotes.
* Assisting V.P. Controller in preparation of interim and year end audit schedules and special projects.

In addition, also responsible for coordination of general accounting function for monthly closing and supervision of data processing operaton.

Major accomplishments:
* Conversion of outside service bureau operations to in-house computer operations and thereby cutting down costs.
* Designed and implemented information flow and reports layout for computerizing sales backlog analysis & accounts payable resulting in better information and savings on costs.

Bakers Brothers, Inc.   August 1973 to July 1976.

Manufacturer of dental/medical cabinetry and home and office furniture. Sales $8 MM.

Assistant Controller/SR Accountant.

Job Responsibilities:
* Administration and supervision of general accounting and cost department functions.
* Development and preparation of manufacturing budgets.
* Assist the controller in Accounts Analysis for external auditors.

Major Accomplishments:
* Developed and installed effective job cost system which led to major improvements in pricing.

Chief Cost Accountant/Div. Commercial Officer with two major companies located in Bombay, India, during August 1960 to April 1973.

EDUCATION
M.B.A. - Finance, Univ. of Tennessee - 1975
D.M.A. - Mgt. Acctg., Univ. of Bombay, India - 1972
M.S. - Cost Acctg., Univ. of Bombay, India - 1964
B.A. - Accounting, Univ. of Bombay, India - 1960

Affiliation: National Association of Accountants
References: Upon Request

Janice Ann Halliday
3487 Peace Grove Drive
Atlanta, Georgia 30341

Telephone: (404) 321-4573

JOB GOAL Graphics Composition Specialist

EXPERIENCE

1985-present **Georgia Pacific Insurance, Atlanta, Georgia**
Graphics Specialist

Handled work assignments that included statistical reports, booklets, brochures, manuals, slides, and promotional materials. Operated magnetic tape selectric composer system, as well as the electronic standalone composer, in the preparation of layout work which varied from rough draft materials to more complex layouts. Used drawing pen for line work of all kinds. Work required the use of judgment in copy marking and entering format instructions into the system output and in determining appropriate spacing and finished layout.

1981-1985 **Murray Wood and Paper Company, Atlanta, Georgia**
Statistical Typist/MT/ST Operator

Typed a variety of statistical reports, sales forecasts, and charts. Received special training on MT/ST, Composer and MT/SC equipment and the drawing pen. Acquired knowledge of type designs and layout fundamentals during a period of two years as a trainee and then as a specialist.

1979-1981 **Georgia Power and Light Company, Atlanta, Georgia**
Clerk Typist

Typed invoices, performed routine clerical tasks and maintained files. Typed from copy and developed statistical skills. Typed charts and statistics for the annual report to stockholders.

EDUCATION

1979 — Certified at Woods Business School
1978 — Graduated from Lee High School

References on request.

ERIC JORGENSEN
555 Middlevale Avenue
Middlevale, New York 13406
716-828-1132

OBJECTIVE

To serve as Chief Administrator
of rural general hospital.

EXPERIENCE

1981-present   Chief Administrator, Riverdale General Hospital,
Riverdale, Montana. Directed all administrative
functions of this 250-bed hospital. Established
all policies, supervised operation of administrative departments (with three assistant administrators). Supervised both professional and nonprofessional personnel, budgeting, special projects,
training logistics. Represented the hospital in
all community affairs and health activities.

1979-1981   Hospital Administrator, Chelsea General Hospital,
Chelsea, Ohio. Directed the activities of all
supervisors, developed more efficient admissions
procedures and developed a public relations-
oriented staff training program, and greatly
improved the overall atmosphere of the hospital
as well as its status in the vicinity.

1977-1979   Assistant Hospital Administrator, Bronx Military
Hospital, Bronx, Indiana. Conferred with Chief
Administrator on all phases of hospital administration, including patient admission procedures,
allocation of office and ward space; interviewed
and selected personnel, and in general had responsibility for efficient operation in all departments
of this 200-bed hospital and all aspects of patient
comfort and rehabilitation.

EDUCATION

Master's degree in Hospital Administration, June
1976, Allentown Medical College, Allentown, Wisconsin, with one-year administrative residence at
Levittown County Hospital in Allentown.

B.S. - 1973, Allentown University - Chemistry Major.

REFERENCES   Will be furnished upon request.

COSETTE LANDER

125 South 10th Street
Philadelphia, PA 19124
215/ 685-7941

Objective

Position as housekeeper/dietitian in
resort hotel or motel requiring supervisory ability and offering full
maintenance

Experience:

9/81-present   **Housekeeper/Dietitian**   Fulton House Motel,
Bala Cynwyd, PA.

Direct staff of 40 porters and maids;
responsible for recruiting and supervising staff of summer college student
personnel; purchase all supplies and
equipment.

1978-1981   **Dietitian**   Henry Hudson Hotel, Port Jervis,
NY .

Responsible for planning menus and supervising 5-person kitchen; functioned as
hostess and supervised 5 waiters and 4
busboys.

Education:

                 B.S. Cornell University, Ithaca, NY .
                 Major: Home Economics
1977   Minor: English

References on request.

Paul Reynolds
25 Bayside Avenue
Seneca, New York 14547
(716) 493-9675

Job Objective   Supervisory position in insurance adjusting

Experience

9/81-present   Claims Adjuster
                     National Insurance Company
                     Seneca, New York
                     Responsible for making on-the-scene investi-
                     gations, obtaining statements from witnesses,
                     assessing property damage, determining liability
                     and negotiating settlement.

6/70-6/81   Office Claims Representative
                     Standard Insurance Company
                     Ithaca, New York
                     Duties included receiving claim forms, con-
                     firming coverage and issuing settlement draft.

7/68-5/70   Property Damage Trainee
                     Acme Casualty Company
                     Watkins Glen, New York
                     Duties included inspecting material damage,
                     obtaining photos, preparing property damage
                     estimates and obtaining agreed prices with
                     body repair shops.

Education

1966-1968   Laraby Junior College, Elmira, New York

References   Available upon request.

Jay Oliver   Home Phone: (512) 203–5681
685 Summer Street   Business Phone: (512) 986–2384
Austin, Texas 78745

Career Objective: Interior Decorator

Experience: Interior Decorator—J and B Decorators, Austin, Texas
6/80–present   Client contact to determine decorating tastes and choices for
                     homes and apartments; submitted sketches and color choices;
                     responsible for shopping, installing, and supervising painters,
                     carpenters, etc.

1/75–5/80   Dispatcher—C.B. Temporaries, Austin, Texas
                     Interviewed applicants, took orders from client companies,
                     dispatched proper temporary to each assignment, assisted in
                     bookkeeping.

Education: University of Texas
1971–1975   B.A. Degree, Art Major

References: Available on request.

Patricia Jones
15 Cayaka Street
Los Angeles, California   90057
(213) 542-5625

Experience:
2/86-present   **Investigator**, J & J, Inc., Los Angeles,
                    California. Function as field investigator
                    to determine the underwriting acceptability
                    for insurance companies, investigate prospec-
                    tive employees for client employers, interview
                    claimants with regard to insurance claim.
                    Dictate cases to secretarial pool.

8/80-2/86   **Inspector**, Los Angeles Credit Company, Los
                    Angeles, California. Inspect property to be
                    insured to ascertain that property is as
                    stated in the insurance application; respon-
                    sible for photographing and sketching such
                    property.

Education: Los Angeles High School
1980   Los Angeles, California

References: Available upon request.

KEYPUNCH OPERATOR

Judy Lee Foster
56 Highland Avenue
Louisville, Kentucky 40223
Telephone: (502) 498-8874

Job Objective - Key Punch Supervisor

Experience

1983-1989   Key Punch Operator: Blue Grass Enterprises, Inc. - Louisville, Ky.

Worked under the direction of the Group Head transcribing data
from source documents to punched cards, following standardized
procedures and instructions. Learned to handle jobs without
specific instructions. Operated alphabetical and numerical
key punch and key verifier machines with speed and accuracy.
Located on the source document the items to be punched and often
had to decipher illegible ones and prepare new ones. Assisted
other operators who were in training.

1981-1983   Transcribing Machine Operator: Colonel Harvey Foods - Louisville,
Ky.

Typed a variety of recorded material, including complex, technical
and sometimes confidential reports. Required to make the proper
choice of layout and form and to be sure punctuation and grammar
were correct.

1979-1981   Clerk Typist: Turtle Manufacturing Company - Lexington, Ky.

Used dictaphone to type letters; typed reports from typewritten
drafts. Did some statistical typing and typed invoices and
purchase orders. Answered call director and helped receptionist.
Operated embossograph to cut name plates and used adding machine.

1978-1979   File Clerk: First National Bank - Lexington, Ky.

Arranged, sorted and filed invoices, correspondence and other
miscellaneous material. Retrieved and refiled items as requested.
Performed some typing assignments.

Education

Lexington Mason High School, Business Studies Diploma, 1978

References

Provided on request.

PHYLLIS FRIED
16 Lakeview Drive
Port Jervis, NY 12416
(914) 682-4184
(914) 680-4260

OBJECTIVE

Management training position in Laboratory Management

EDUCATION

BS in Behavioral Science, Summa Cum Laude. GPA 4.0
Union College, Middletown, NY, June 1986
Certificates in Human Behavior & Personnel Management

AAS, Medical Technology, June 1965
Westchester Community College, Valhalla, NY

EXPERIENCE

Aerovistes, Port Jervis, NY   1983-Present
   Laboratory Manager
   -Assisted lab director in creation of commercial
    laboratory
   -Interact with director and sales manager in developing
    marketing strategies
   -Designed and assisted in implementation of
    computerized reporting and record keeping system
   -Oversee daily operatons

Port Jervis Hospital Center, Port Jervis, NY   1979-83
   Medical Technologist
   -Functioned in all areas of the laboratory
   -Assisted department head in providing emergency
    toxicology service

Scranton Hospital, Scranton, PA   1967-77
   Blood Bank Supervisor
   -Was primarily responsible for daily operations of
    transfusion service
   -Assisted in donor recruitment

SPECIAL SKILLS

Working knowledge of various word processing systems and
other personal computer applications.

REFERENCES

Available upon request.

Harry R. Leason
6789 Vander Drive
Lemon Grove, California 92045

Will relocate

(805) 657-8934

Job Objective: Senior Laboratory Technician

Experience

Ace-Hunt Pet Food Company, Fullerton, California

Skilled Technician
1979-present

Carried out specialized, complex, non-repetitive experiments requiring extensive knowledge of the technology involved. Performed routine experiments, operated experimental equipment, and produced experimental samples of materials according to established quality standards. Assigned to lead a group of less experienced technicians (college recruits) in specific assignments. Communicated results of assignments within the established format.

Laboratory Technician
1977-1979

Performed varied routine tests required and prepared samples. Set up and operated laboratory equipment such as colorimeter, spectrophotometer, refractometer, microscopes, mixers, dryers, grinders, filters and the enlarging and contact apparatus for photographic work.

Laboratory Assistant
1975-1977

Worked under the supervision of the Group Leader performing simple chemical and physical test routines. Assisted in the assembly and set up of equipment; prepared standard test solutions and regimens; recorded test data; and as required, performed routine detailed work in the research and development laboratories as requested by the professional staff. Kept laboratory clean and in good order and handled and cared for small animals.

Education

Lemon Grove High School. Received diploma in 1975.

Won Lemon Grove Science Competition Award in 1973.

References

On request.

SUSAN STEIN
118 W. 79
New York, New York 10056
212-864-4215

EXPERIENCE:

**June 1983-
Present**

Bertram Goldstein, P.C., New York, New York

<u>Law Clerk in bankruptcy practice</u>. Responsibilities include research of bankruptcy and related matters, writing memos, drafting of letters and court pleadings.

**January 1983-
June 1983**

Israel, Krasner and Madison, New York, New York

<u>Law Clerk with general practice firm</u>. Duties included research, drafting, pleadings for various cases dealing with Immigration, Negligence, and Contract Law. Handled court filings and client interviews.

**September 1982-
January 1983**

Paine Webber Jackson, Curtis & Co., Inc., New York, New York

<u>Assistant Broker</u>. Solicited new accounts for various municipal and stock funds.

**October 1980-
August 1982**

Morgan Guaranty Trust Company, New York, New York

<u>Corporate Trust Administrator</u>. Reviewed indentures, mortgages, and other financing documents for accounts of $1 million or more. Responsible for payments and investments on various trust accounts. Reviewed company compliance with financial trust agreements.

**March 1980-
September 1980**

Stein and Day Publishers, New York, New York

<u>Publicity Assistant</u>. Organized author tours, wrote press releases for all major media. Handled daily managerial functions of the publicity department.

**July 1979-
March 1980**

John L. Burns, Jr., New York, New York

<u>Personal Aide</u>. Acted as an assistant press secretary for W.I.S.E. (lobby group). Assisted in the organization and management of the opening of the Adeline Moses Burns Gallery at the Fraunces Tavern. Also acted as a political aide on Mr. Burns' Exploratory Committee for Federal Office. Responsibilities included all media and public contact as well as various research projects.

(Continued)

EDUCATION:

August 1984-   Attending CUNY Law School.
Present   Participant in Law School's Judicial Clinic during Fall
                    Semester of 1985, assigned to the Criminal Justice
                    Institute. Duties included legal research and preparation
                    of written memorandum. In spring of 1985, assigned to
                    Chief Judge Conrad Duberstein of The United States
                    Bankruptcy Court in the Eastern District of New York.
                    Duties included legal research and preparation of
                    written memorandum.

September 1978-   Attended Fordham University.
May 1982   Received B.A. History and Political Science. Honors
                    include Dean's List and graduating cum laude. Campus
                    editor of university-wide newspaper, member of student
                    government, member of College Council and Financial
                    Aid Committee.

                              References available upon request.

Elizabeth R. Jonas
3450 Downer Road
Seattle, Washington, 98116

Telephone: (206) 576–8934

Job Objective: Corporate Librarian

Experience

1980–present

Marketing Librarian
Oakland Electronics Corporation — Seattle, Washington

Maintain Marketing Library providing extensive source material for marketing personnel and a marketing information service to operating divisions. Issue a bulletin periodically listing new publications, articles and studies on marketing as well as competitive new products.

Research, summarize and submit comprehensive information on all areas related to the corporation's interests, from secondary sources and outside contacts. Keep statistical tables on population and socioeconomic trends, consumption and prices; other demographics. Maintain comprehensive and up-to-date information and constantly add to any update holdings.

Establish and maintain continuing relationships with sources of information (government bureaus, consulates of foreign countries, trade associations, trade and consumer press, special libraries, and public libraries) through phone calls, visits, correspondence, and attendance at library association meetings.

1978–1980

Assistant Librarian
Holt, Wagner and Smith Investment Brokerage — Seattle, Washington

Scanned periodicals and referred specific articles to interested personnel. Clipped and filed items of permanent value. Cataloged books, maintained library files and revised when necessary, handled routine requests for material, and checked listings of new material in trade press, outside sources, and govenment bulletins. Ordered books. pamphlets, magazines as needed to keep the library collection updated.

Education

University of Oregon — B.S. degree Library Science — 1977

References

Will be provided on request.

Henry O'Connor
145-96 Smart Street
Chicago, Illinois 44498
(315) 598-9987

Experience:

March 11, 1984 to Present	Charles Booker, Inc. Stock Brokerage
	97 Lake Michigan Drive
	Chicago, Illinois 44493

Currently Purchasing Manager responsible for office
supplies which include stationery, envelopes,
departmental forms, bank checks, etc.; printing,
all in-house and outside vender contracts; furniture and machines (i.e.,Pitney Bowes, UARCO,
Addressograph, Xerox and IBM); and all maintenance
contracts relating to the latter.

Responsibilities also include managing the Mail
Department which has a staff of eight. The Mail
Department handles all incoming and outgoing mail,
daily confirmations, monthly statements, printing
on a 1250 Multilith, UARCO disbursements and inventory control (Burster and Delever machines).

Through varied experience in purchasing and line
management, have implemented inventory control
procedures. Currently using manual forms to
control all levels of inventory. Current inventory
control procedures tie in purchasing, inventory
management, reordering surplus and equipment evaluation as a unique separate function. Have developed
contacts with outside venders and have initiated
blanket order contracts to create savings for the
firm.

December, 1973
to
March 8, 1984

Blackman and Miller Co., Inc.   Stock Brokerage
48-07 Bank Street
Chicago, Illinois 44492

Duties were exactly the same as stated above. Firm
went into liquidation.

June, 1969
to
December, 1973

Cassidy, Newman, Bright and Eli   Stock Brokerage
755 East 8th Street
Chicago, Illinois 44497

Duties were basically the same as stated above.

References: Will be supplied upon request.

MARTHA BANKS
100 Center Street
Chicago, IL 61415
(213) 815-4225

CAREER
OBJECTIVE:

Seeking an entry level position in the field of Management with preference in Marketing.

EDUCATION:

Syracuse University, Syracuse, New York
Bachelor of Science, May 1989
School of Management
Majors: Marketing
          Transportation and Physical
          Distribution

LANGUAGES:

Bilingual: English and Spanish

QUALIFICATIONS:

ADMINISTRATIVE SKILLS
*   Performed analysis of accounts, invoicing of local and international accounts.
*   Issued payroll checks for Inca Land Tours, Cuzco.
*   Maintained journal on client contacts and services.
*   Negotiated contracts with hotels, passenger carriers, tour guides and other travel agencies.
*   Planned and programmed individual and group package tours.
*   Recorded and filed memberships for the Spanish Professionals in America.

SUPERVISORY SKILLS
*   Assisted in setting up and organizing three travel agencies in Peru.
*   Coordinated the responsibilities of the agencies and their employees.
*   Instructed international students (elementary school) as a bilingual teacher assistant.

COMMUNICATIVE SKILLS
*   Experienced customer contact as sales clerk in Dey Brothers Stores (Syracuse), and as tours sales representative for ILT Lima International.
*   Performed social and personal assistance to families and students enrolled in the English as a Second Language Program (Syracuse).

(Continued)

       *   Tutored private students in Spanish and
            Literature.
       *   Translated for the International
            Division at L.B. Smith Co.
       *   Constant contact with patrons at the
            Syracuse University Mathematics Library
            as an assistant librarian.

<u>WORK HISTORY</u>:
9/87-5/89   S.U. Mathematics Library--Librarian-assistant
8/86-3/87   ALDEEU Spanish Professionals in America--
                 Secretary
                 Syracuse City School District--Teacher
                 Assistant ESL.
9/82-10/83   Dey Brothers Stores (Syracuse)--Sales Clerk
10/79-5/81   Inca Land Tours S.A. (Peru)--Promotion and
                 International Sub-manager.

<u>REFERENCES</u>:   Available on request.

BRUCE CAMPBELL
2100 Broadway
New York, N.Y. 10023

212 SU 7-4210

OBJECTIVE: To relocate to suburban area with position as Manager of Research or Advertising in a small publishing company.

EXPERIENCE

1983-present   Manager, Advertising and Sales Promotion, Carlton Publications, New York, N.Y. In charge of all phases inherent in publication of six trade magazines with nationwide distribution to industrial corporations.

1982-1983   Manager, Advertising and Sales Promotion, Collins Research Corporation, Bear Lake, New York. Directed all operations involved in advertising and sales promotion, with staff of eight, in this company which produced electrical meters and various electrical components used in radios and television sets.

1981-1982   Advertising Manager, Hersey-Starling Electronics Division, New York, N.Y. Integrated and supervised activities involved in publicity and sales promotion of products, including transistors, receivers, television picture tubes, digital display devices and digital integrated circuits.

1971-1981   Manager, Advertising and Sales Promotion, William Meyers Associates, New York, N.Y. Organized and executed advertising and sales presentation programs for the promotion of this company's products which included pipe fittings and meter valves, thermostats and various control devices.

1968-1971   Valve Design Engineer, Marine Motors, Seagirt, Long Island. Designed valves for use in marine equipment. Conducted research for improvement in design and construction of these valves.

(Continued)

2

Bruce Campbell   Manager, Advertising and
                                            Sales Promotion

EXPERIENCE (cont'd.)

1966-1968   Assistant Project Engineer, Cylinder Design Dept.,
                 Curtis Motor Design Corporation, Alison, NJ.
                 Made blueprints and sketches of original designs
                 for motor cylinders, for cars, trucks and tractors.
                 Investigated and corrected design imperfections in
                 cylinders already in operation in motor vehicles,
                 for more efficient functioning.

EDUCATION

   B.S. in Automotive Engineering, 1966 - Pace Polytechnic Institute

PUBLICATIONS

   Series of five articles on investigative research into the causes
   of malfunction, and correction of defective auto parts, published
   in *Automotive America*, January-May issues, 1974.

REFERENCES

   References on request.

THOMAS LUDWIG
29 Rockland Ave.
Yonkers, NY 12028
(914) 448-1269

Education	M.B.A. Program (1973), University of Kentucky; 27 hours of business prerequisites and 9 hours of graduate work
	New York University, M.A.; 1972
	St. Louis University, A.B. magna cum laude; 1970
Professional Experience	City Bank Co., New York, New York
1978-present	Position: Manager, Timesharing Services (2/81 to Present)

Supervision of a group of 6 people with responsibility for technical support and user interface for in-house timesharing systems (600 users); coordination of the use of outside timesharing services (500 users). Timesharing billing, and the provision of consulting services in various applications to the timesharing community. Now working on a 2-year plan for consolidation of all time sharing on a dedicated in-house system.

Position: Manager Software Products (1978 to 1981)

Supervision of a group of 9 people with responsibility for the implementation and maintenance of an interactive programming development system using VM/CMS, installation and support of user-related program products (compilers, utilities, etc.), technical support for all applications groups within Banker's Trust, and installation and support of TI and DEC software. Had major project responsibility for the VM/CMS system from planning to implementation; project completed on time and within budget.

1974-1978	WESTERN UNION, St. Louis, Missouri

Position: Senior Systems Analyst

Responsible for all computing: 2 major systems, computer-assisted instruction, research projects, and hardware and software planning. Supervised 5 people.

1973-1974	XTRA CORPORATION, Chicago, Illinois

Position: Standards and Education Manager

Responsible for standards and education of all applications programming groups and for evaluation and selection of software packages.

REFERENCES FURNISHED UPON REQUEST

James Rivera
15 Maple Street
Youngstown, Ohio 44575
(216) 765-7035 home
(216) 765-6229 work

EMPLOYMENT

7/83–present   U.S. RUBBER CO., INC.   Youngstown, Ohio

Marketing Research Analyst. Responsible for providing objective and reliable information to senior management, with data obtained from pre-and post-product surveys, marketing program evaluations, pricing studies, and advertising and merchandising research projects. Developed new computer pricing programs for competitive pricing analysis and risk analysis simulation. Directed research staff for survey programs. Conducted major metropolitan market evaluations for sales personnel training.

7/82–7/83   GENERAL TIRE AND RUBBER   Akron, Ohio

District Manager—Dealer Sales. Responsible for dealer sales of tires and related products in Ohio and western Pennsylvania. Sales quota attainment $3,000,000+. Developed and trained new and existing independent dealers. Assisted dealers in all financial and operational functions.

5/81–7/82   REYNOLDS RUBBER CORPORATION   Detroit, Michigan

Product Marketing Associate. Assisted in the development of the marketing plans for passenger, light truck, and performance tires. Developed new product marketing plans, sales strategies, and sales forecasts for the Comp T/A tire line. Created a computer assisted regression analysis forecasting system for all new product lines. Assembled and computed daily sales and inventory analysis reports. Conducted marketing strategy review meetings. Developed and implemented special task force programs for new products.

1979–1980   J. & G. MARSHALL ASSOCIATES   Dearborn, Michigan

Industrial Coordinator. Responsible for the design, manufacturing, and packaging of industrial hardware. Organized and executed product installation at customers' premises.

Summers 1978–1979   BICYCLES UNLIMITED   Bloomington, Indiana

Co-Owner and Operator. Responsible for advertising, bidding, hiring, training, supervising employees, and maintaining financial records. Company grossed $25,000 to $30,000 per summer. Paid for all college tuition and additional expenses.

EDUCATION
1979   B.S., University of Indiana, Bloomington

REFERENCES   Furnished upon request.

CARLETON K. ROBERTS
16 Bell Street
Harris, Minnesota 55941
Telephone: 218-583-9313

OBJECTIVE: Result- and profit-motivated innovative marketer
with accomplishments in Corporate Market and
Economic Research, Marketing Management
Consulting, Market Development.
Target Corporate Development.

EXPERIENCE:

SENIOR MARKET
RESEARCH ANALYST   FAL CORPORATION, New Falls, Minnesota
1984-present

Responsible to the Manager of Market Research for
collection and analysis of information in business
areas of interest to the corporation. Survey and
evaluate literature and interpret trends where
relevant. Organize investigations, analyze, report
findings and recommendations to management.

Recommended a course of action for establishing R&D
objective. Researched and developed a half billion
dollar market related to current product lines.
Market segmentation pinpointed R&D goals.

Suggest market opportunities, consult on new
products, evaluate production and supply statistics.
Interpret economic news.

SENIOR ANALYST   JOHNSON AND CO., INC., Raleigh, SC 1976-1984

Engaged in all functional responsibilities necessary
to answering critical questions for Fortune 500
clients. Advanced from Market Analyst to Senior
Associate. Developed more than 50 major studies
calculated to have yielded millions of dollars to
corporate customers.

Studies were sponsored to: audit and define consumer
and industrial markets; help plan and test new
products and services; evaluate sales and
distribution operations; appraise acquisitions or
divestitures; plan production facilities proximate
to markets, etc.

(Continued)

CARLETON K. ROBERTS
Page 2

        Personal research has effectively:

- Evaluated the distributor network of a proposed 15 million dollar corporate acquisition.
- Determined the advisability of a client divesting a 10 million dollar sales division.
- Delineated the market for production of a proposed 19 million dollar turnkey process facility.
- Measured share of market and isolated areas for penetration for a 100 million dollar supplier of specialty materials.
- Developed statistical and qualitative audits of industries segmenting profitability of product markets. Used by sponsors to plan multi-million dollar productions and define goals.

FIELD UNDERWRITER   STATE INSURANCE, Greg Plains, Nebraska

Marketed personal lines of coverages. Trained and received New York State licensing. Conducted telephone and in-person prospecting. Sold concepts and underwrote life, health, and disability protection and/or to meet estate plans.

SALES MANAGER   FIELD BROS. IMPORTERS LTD., N.Y., N.Y.

Administered territorial sales and marketing activities. Successfully motivated the several forms of customers to stock and promote sales of a broad line of packaged goods. Cultivated associated distributor personnel's cooperation and gained their interest in promoting coverage and sales volume.

Achieved near saturation distribution in a market containing over 2,000 accounts. Was successful in converting this near virgin territory to a highly profitable market with improved volume of over 800%.

Projected company policies, sales supports and product uniqueness to the industry and in distributor meetings.

EDUCATION: B.B.A., Major Economics, University of Miami, Coral Gables, Florida, 1973

REFERENCES: Available upon request.

CATHERINE BROOKS
Bedford Hills Drive
Austin, Texas 75203
(241) 891-3015
(241) 685-5000

CAREER OBJECTIVE:	To secure a position in marketing or marketing related field that will enable me to expand my areas of responsibilities with further career potential.
EXPERIENCE: 4/79 - Present	Austin Medical Services Austin, Texas
4/83 - Present	Marketing Coordinator/Patient Relations

Responsibilities:

- Gather and analyze research and campaign results in order to develop future marketing plans

- Coordinate and implement marketing efforts involving executive staff, field operations and advertising agency

- Interface with advertising agency on the day-to-day activities of media production, ad approvals, placements and billings

- Direct and manage patient relations and surveys

- Interview employees and write all internal news releases involving moves and changes within the organization

- Establish and implement centralized purchasing systems for ten locations

- Report directly to General Manager on special marketing and operational projects requiring research and analysis

8/80-4/83   Executive Secretary/Office Manager

Responsibilities:

- Support services for top-level management during division's start-up phase

- Personnel Administration

- Meeting and travel planning

- Supervise secretarial support team

4/79 - 8/80   Senior Secretary

3/75 - 6/77	Dr. Theodore Marks Austin, Texas
Position:	Secretary/Receptionist
EDUCATION: 1/81 - 12/82	Baylor University Major Course Study - Marketing
REFERENCES:	Furnished upon request

Wayne Johnson
10 Morris Street
Elmhurst, NY 11340
(718) 968-3279

OCCUPATIONAL GOAL	Marketing Management Trainee
JOB OBJECTIVE	Trainee in marketing-related area such as advertising, marketing research, or public relations with the possibility of advancing to a position of more responsibility in marketing management.
EXPERIENCE	Worked an average of 30 hours a week to help pay for college.
1984-1989	MACY'S INC., White Plains, N.Y.
	Started as salesperson and was promoted to Department Sponsor. Responsibilities included scheduling lunches and breaks, authorizing exchanges and refunds, making cash deposits, setting up ads and special promotions, planning floor moves, and aiding in the taking of inventory. Managed area in manager's absence for three months. Received outstanding compliments from buyers and administrators for work done.
1982-1984	ALEXANDER'S, White Plains, N.Y.
	Salesperson in men's division. Promoted to Sunday and night supervisor after one year. Duties included scheduling breaks, setting up ads and special promotions, authorizing exchanges and refunds, training new employees, and supervising ten employees.
EDUCATION	MERCY COLLEGE
	Bachelor of Science in Business Administration with specialization in Management (May 1989) Magna Cum Laude. Cum. 3.6
	HONORS
	Dean's List, four semesters
SKILLS	Foreign Language: French
	Programming Language: BASIC

BARRY WESTIN
52-32 Sycamore Street
Forest Hills, New York 11375   212-345-6731

EXPERIENCE

1983-present Production Manager, Ronson Management Research, Inc.,
              New York City. P/L responsibility for $500,000
              marketing budget used in direct mail, space advertis-
              ing and telephone sales. Wrote annual marketing
              plans and forecasted product pro-forma statements.
              Doubled 1974 revenues to $1.6 million by segmenting
              existing markets and pinpointing new ones. Inte-
              grated marketing and financial data to rank markets
              according to profitability. Heavily used cost
              accounting and advanced marketing research techniques.
              Supervised copywriters, artists, printers and media
              buyers in advertising and sales promotion campaigns.

1982-1983   Marketing Research Analyst, Rolands Mail Order House,
              Milwaukee, Wisc. Developed statistical program for
              evaluating new customer credit applications. Used
              analysis of variance techniques to correlate customer
              demographics with payment history. Determined opti-
              mal mailing sequence for catalog and direct mail
              response. Determined user needs. Wrote MIS specifi-
              cations for corporate programming staff.

EDUCATION

1982-1983   Graduate School of Business, Milwaukee University,
              M.B.A. Concentrated in Marketing and Financial
              Management. Secondary interests in Organizational
              Development.

1977-1982   University of Detroit. B.S. degree.
              Majored in Systems Analysis Engineering and Opera-
              tions Research.

HONORS   Recipient of Astor Scholarship at Milwaukee
              University, and Michigan State and Morgansteiner
              Scholarships at University of Detroit. Graduated
              with honors.

LANGUAGES   Speak both French and German fluently.

References   Available upon request.

MARKETING MANAGER

Travor Hill Johnson
214 Main Street
Charleston, West Virginia 25201
(304) 357-8075

Education: <u>University of Chicago</u>, Chicago, Illinois. Received M.B.A. in June, 1985. Work included four courses in marketing, including marketing management, family consumer behavior, market research and international marketing; financial and cost accounting; macroeconomics and microeconomics; investments; calculus; linear programming and statistics. M.B.A. work also provided experience with an interactive data analysis system in statistics and exposure to systems analysis and basic assembly language.

<u>Union College</u>, Schenectady, New York. Received B.A. in American Studies in June, 1982. Course work included sociology, history, economics, literature and psychology oriented to the study of American culture and group life. Senior Thesis on subject of the ideals of cooperation and competition in American educational thought. Involved in committee to strengthen American Studies program at Union. Dean's List. Completed course work in three years.

Work Experience:

February, 1986
to
present

<u>The Commonwealth Group</u>, Stamford, Connecticut. Consultant. Responsible for design and execution of marketing study for a Connecticut bank interested in the Stamford business community. Project includes internal and external interviews and extensive competitive analysis to arrive at a positioning for the bank and other recommendations about Stamford operations. Also involved in certain stages of new business activities and analysis of other consulting projects.

June to
September, 1985

<u>AMF Alcort</u>, Waterbury, Connecticut. Consultant. Gathered and interpreted statistical and other data related to the present and potential markets for the Sunfish sailboat to determine the product's annual sales potential nationwide. Worked with corporate, Marine Products Group and Alcort personnel.

Autumn, 1984

<u>David Overton Associates</u>, Barrington, Illinois. Consultant. Constructed cost model for the packaging, transportation and distribution of a consumer product on a regional basis. Involved in developing marketing plans for product. Work done on a consulting basis while in business school.

Summer, 1983

<u>Alan Wood Steel</u>, Conshohocken, Pennsylvania. Mill clerk in cold mill. Maintained production and other statistics.

Summer, 1982

<u>Vocational Adjustment Center</u>, South Boston, Mass. Work involved supervising retardates in behavior-modification setting.

References: Available upon request.

MARY SOKOLOV
19 Mystic Road
Lancaster, Pennsylvania 17603
(717) 955–4083

PROFESSIONAL OBJECTIVE:

Seeking an outstanding opportunity in national marketing/sales that will utilize my years of experience in these areas as a consistently high achiever who is highly motivated, well educated, and totally sales oriented.

REGIONAL MARKETING MANAGER

Bradley Electronics, Inc., Lancaster, Pennsylvania   1980–Present

Manufacturer and distributor of computer-based products and services.
Promoted into position within one year assuming managerial responsibility for a major division of a newly established company that used my marketing and sales skills.

- Increased sales volume more than 49% each consecutive year in a highly competitive market.
- Responsible for a sales division which has generated a tripling of sales and profits for a three year period.
  - Staffed and trained outside sales force
  - Became a resource person, trouble shooter, and closer for sales staff
  - Initiated telemarketing program including staffing and training personnel setting up successful incentive plan
  - Created and wrote individualized proposals
- Developed sales and marketing strategies
  - Designed brochures, demonstration kits, advertising, direct mailings
  - Input into product design

MARKETING REPRESENTATIVE

Lancaster Laboratories, Philadelphia, Pa.   1975–1980

Sold mechanical equipment, supplies, drugs and medicines to physicians. In conjunction with attending school in order to finance my education, I worked part time until graduation and then assumed the position full time.

- Enlarged markets for established and new products which resulted in a substantial increase in new accounts.

OTHER:

INDEPENDENT CONSULTANT of computer systems and peripherals utilizing my background in developing accounting and marketing systems for the business client. 1987 to Present.

EDUCATION:

B.S. ACCOUNTING/MARKETING, Scranton University, Scranton, Pennsylvania, 1975

WILLING TO RELOCATE

REFERENCES WILL BE FURNISHED UPON REQUEST

CARLA D'ANGELO
2851 Buhre Avenue
Bronx, New York 10461
(212) 823-4735

CAREER OBJECTIVE
To obtain an entry level management position in a firm with growth potential.

EDUCATION:
FORDHAM UNIVERSITY
Bronx, New York
Bachelor of Science in Marketing
Cumulative Major Index: 3.0
September 1984 to May 1989

EMPLOYMENT HISTORY:
SAKS FIFTH AVENUE (offices)
Yonkers, New York
Position: Security Officer
July 1985 to Present

-Maintaining safety of employees
-Protecting a National Distribution Complex
-Training of new security officers
-Performing internal audits
-Producing surveillance and loss prevention reports
-Tracing merchandise and interstore transfers via On-Line
 Cathode Ray Tube computer terminal

S.K. MERCHANDISE
Bronx, New York
Position: Order Clerk
November 1984 to July 1985

-Processed purchase orders for office supplies
-Made appropriate adjustments to accommodate customers

GRISTEDE'S SUPERIOR FOODS
New York, New York
Position: Stock Clerk
October 1982 to November 1984

-Provided direct customer services
-Performed various clerical duties

REFERENCES FURNISHED UPON REQUEST

Anthony T. Falk   Telephone: (918) 529-3309
569 59th Avenue
Tulsa, Oklahoma   74105

Job Objective: Marketing/Sales Director

Experience   King Regan Corp., Tulsa, Oklahoma
1980-present   Assistant to President

                 Directed the marketing for new products in the freeze-dried
                 field. Researched the market and competition, test-marketed
                 products and trained sales force for national distribution.
                 Followed the successful distribution of products on consumer
                 level with the training of institutional sales staff to open
                 key institutional accounts.

                 Found new markets for established products and opened
                 European distribution for U.S. products. Developed sales
                 and marketing strategy, searched for and identified specific
                 markets and developed methods of penetrating those markets.

                 Responsibility for advertising, packaging, promotions and
                 product development.

1978-1980   Crowley Industrial Bag Inc., Cleveland, Ohio
                 Marketing Director

                 Responsibility for diversification to consumer products,
                 opening key accounts, directing new technology. Utilized
                 market research methods, impact point of purchase pieces
                 and both product and corporate advertising to launch the
                 consumer products. Worked closely with package designers
                 to develop unified packaging with a hard-sell profile.
                 Supervised training of a special sales force.

1975-1978   Ace Marine Supplies and Boats, Chicago, Illinois
                 Product Manager

                 Created new markets for established products and recommended
                 product improvements. To capitalize on the growing demand
                 for fiber glass boats, worked with designers to make changes
                 in our 40-foot yacht to create a 40-foot motor sailboat.
                 The market followed our trend and sales more than doubled over
                 sales on the original yacht in the line in previous years.

                                                                 (Continued)

1973-1975   Chicago Sun Times, Chicago, Illinois
                   Salesman _____

                   Sold classified and display advertising in local market.

Education   1973 M.B.A. degree from University of Chicago.

                   Graduated 1970 from Xavier University with B.S. and B.A.
                   degrees in Economics and Accounting.

References   On request.

George Adams
10 Waters Road
Santa Fe, NM 87124
(505) 371-0200

OBJECTIVE   Senior Sales or Marketing position with major Software
             Vendor.

EDUCATION   North Texas State University, B.A. Mathematics; 1967

EMPLOYMENT HISTORY

1981-   Software Systems of North America
present   Santa Fe, NM

             As Account Manager, responsibilities included marketing
             DATABASE II and associated products in North Texas and
             Oklahoma and establishing a Dallas office. Attained quota
             of $1.1M, finishing 101% of quota for the year.

1973-1981   Forum Corporation
             Phoenix, AZ

             As Marketing Representative from February 1979-January 1980,
             responsibilities included marketing the entire product line,
             territory planning and management, and revenue forecasting
             and budget control. Ranked Number 2 in the U.S. at 216% of
             quota   ($547,000 in booked business and 7 new systems in-
             stalled).

             Promoted to Senior Marketing Representative. Finished 9-
             month sales period of 1980 with $220,000 in business while
             developing a new territory.

             Was Marketing Representative of the Month in July and Sep-
             tember, 1979. Other positions held were Systems Programmer,
             Systems Engineer, Senior Systems Engineer, District Support
             Manager.

1967-1973   Information Leaders
             El Paso, TX

             As Systems Engineer in Life Insurance Industry Group, was
             responsible for entire Letters and Notices Systems for three
             life insurance accounts; for defining, implementing, and
             coding new letters for existing systems; for maintaining and
             improving existing systems; and for supporting application
             programmers.

References: Available upon request

ANDREW EASTON
10 Tyrolia Avenue
Lawrence, NY 11559

Home Phone: (516) 513-0791
Business: (516) 886-1169

BUSINESS HISTORY

TYLO AND TYLO, INC.

1978 - present · Associate Media Director

Prepared media plans for Lenox China, International Silver, Binney and Smith (Crayola), Loctite, Connecticut Bank and Trust Co., Julius Wile.

CONEDIA AND EVVON, INC.

1972 - 1978 · Media Buyer

Prepared media plans and supervised media research. Handled buying on such accounts as Dutch Boy Paint, Hartford Insurance, Genesee Beer, Snow Crop, and Chun King.

ESTHERSON ASSOCIATES

1961-1972 · Print Media Buyer and Media Specialist (Business Papers)

Prepared media plans and recommendations on magazines, newspapers, and business papers for specific accounts including Continental Can, Armstrong Cork, U.S. Steel, and Du Pont.

Served as a member of the Media Plans Board, which reviewed and made basic recommendations for all accounts. Acted as consultant on business media to many accounts which were basically assigned to other buyers. This included both New York and out-of-town offices, with some contact with virtually every Estherson Associates account.

Served for four years as a member of the Business Paper Committee of the American Association of Advertising Agencies.

1958-1961 · Print Buyer

Wrote media recommendations on specific problems and handled print buying and estimating for Du Pont, T.W.A., and others.

EDUCATION · Haverford College, B.A., 1961.

REFERENCES · Available upon request.

R. S. WATSON
270 Runnymede Street
Lipton, Arkansas 19701

EMPLOYMENT

1983-1989   Jessica Blaine, Inc. -- St. Augustine, Florida

President: activities consisted of planning, account acquisition, creative direction, copy, media selection and related functions.

1982-1983   T. Teaks, Inc. -- Reno, Nevada

Account Executive: complete responsibility for all agency activity on Harcourt Brace Jovanovich, Inc., Subaru Automobiles. Assisted as Account Executive on Singer Fabrics and Notions, plus related agency operations, new business and special projects.

1979-1981   Field and Spring International, Inc. -- Chicago, Illinois

Assistant Account Executive: Eastern Airlines (Broadcast and Print), functioned under the Y and R training program on the following accounts: Dash, Salvo, Gainesburger, Top Choice, Marshall Cavendish Ltd., Travelers Insurance, Liggett & Myers, General Cigar, Pepsico International, British Rail.

1976 - 1979   Uni Med, Inc. -- Chicago, Illinois

Division Chief: responsible for the supervision and coordination of activities of 27 employees in the Group Contracts Division of the Correspondence Department.

EDUCATION

Hofstra University, Hempstead, L.I., New York
B.S., business administration, 1976.

REFERENCES

Will be furnished upon request.

DAVID BENCKE . 300 East 93rd Street . New York, NY 10028 . (212) 737-6620

OBJECTIVE: MEDIA SALES - PRINT/BROADCASTING

SUMMARY: Results-oriented salesman with proven ability for productive effort. Broad background in self-education through employment in different types of industries as well as extensive travel throughout United States, the Caribbean, Latin America and Europe. Excellent verbal skills. Proficient in French. Strong in interpersonal relations.

RELEVANT EXPERIENCE:

1980-present   TREND NEWSPAPERS, INC., Boston, MA
               Account Executive
               *   Serviced established accounts; contacted and sold new accounts

               *   Presented prestige concept of publication to prospects; assisted clients in ad design and composition

               *   Worked with clients in establishing new format for ads when publication changed size from tabloid to magazine

               *   Maintained excellent customer relations with established accounts through reinforcement of magazine concept

               *   Brought in two important accounts in first week

Concurrent   TIME/LIFE LIBRARIES, INC., Boston, MA
               Telephone Sales Representative

               *   Developed sales of Home Improvement Series through phone contact with people in their homes

                    -    Established nineteen new accounts in four days (200 calls, 50 pitches - working four hours per day)

1979   BARNES & NOBLE BOOKSTORE, Boston, MA
(Christmas   Sales Clerk
Season)   *   Maintained company policy of instant and courteous assistance to customers; set up displays for best attraction; helped with inventory

OTHER EXPERIENCE:

1979   73 MAGAZINE, INC., Peterborough, NH
                <u>Book</u> <u>Production</u> <u>Assistant</u>
                *   Edited manuscripts and other copy; proofread
                     and corrected galleys; selected type;
                     produced rough pasteups; participated in
                     research

1972-1978   SUMMERTIME AND PART-TIME JOBS WHILE GOING TO
                SCHOOL

                -    Lumber Industry, Missoula, MT - sawmill
                     assistant
                -    Management Consulting Firm, Durham, NH -
                     groundskeeper
                -    Construction Industry, Lee, NH - swimming
                     pool installation
                -    Laundry Industry, Portsmouth, NH - delivery
                     driver
                -    Prescott Park Arts Festival, Portsmouth, NH -
                     art instructor
                -    Also: crewed on 65 ft. ketch; housepainter,
                     Alaska; landscape gardener; grape harvester
                     in France

EDUCATION: UNIVERSITY OF NEW HAMPSHIRE, Durham, NH
                1978 - BA, English; Minor: French
                ALLIANCE FRANCAISE, Paris, France
                1976 - French

REFERENCES: Available upon request

ALICE RAND
180 Pine St.
Bronxville, NY 12415
(914) 949-4077

OBJECTIVE   Challenging position as a media trainee.

EDUCATION   MONROE COLLEGE, Yonkers, New York
9/87-present   Currently enrolled in program leading to an M.B.A.

                 Concentration in financial management with special emphasis on
                 the study of accounting for management control.

9/83 - 6/87   UNIVERSITY OF FAIRFIELD, Fairfield, Connecticut

                 B.S. Major in Real Estate and Urban Economic Development. Ex-
                 tensive course work in real property appraisal and investment
                 analysis.

EMPLOYMENT   MONROE COLLEGE, Yonkers, New York
9/88-10/88   Assistant to the manager of analytical studies

                 (Six-week internship). Collected synthesized price data for
                 College's annual inflation study. Project involved library research
                 as well as telephone contact with college suppliers. Internship led
                 to current part-time position of coordination draft for final report.

9/85-6/87   UNIVERSITY OF FAIRFIELD, Fairfield, Connecticut

                 Head resident. Responsible for running all aspects of a college
                 dormitory. Duties included supervising residents, kitchen and
                 maintenance staff and preparing all paperwork for Department of
                 Student Affairs. Job was concurrent with full-time academic study
                 to earn seventy percent of college expenses.

SUMMERS

1986   EATON REAL ESTATE, New Canaan, Connecticut

                 Real estate salesperson. Employed part-time by Eaton for buying
                 and selling real property.

1985   MONROE COLLEGE, Yonkers, New York

                 Dispatcher. Employed by physical plant department with respon-
                 sibility for keeping accurate records on thirty-vehicle motor pool.

1984   Groundsperson. Responsible for maintenance of college buildings
                 and grounds.

REFERENCES   Available on request.

Stephanie Andreas
64 London Place
Orange, NJ 07078
(201) 244-9876

Job Objective: To apply my expertise in a medical or hospital lab.

Employment History

    6/73-present   **Medical Technician**

                            St. John's Hospital, Newark, N.J.
                            Responsible for all testing in 300-bed
hospital; supervise 4 lab assistants;
responsible for hospital studies of blood,
skin, urine; assist in radioisotope on
thyroid tests; assist in pathological
studies.

    7/70 - 5/73   **Laboratory Assistant**

                            East Orange General Hospital, East Orange,
N.J. Collected samples and conducted
routine blood tests; conducted prelimi-
nary patient interviews.

Education   B.S., Douglass College, 1970.
Chemistry major, biology minor.

References on request

```
                    MARGIE A. THOMPSON
                    89 WOODRIDGE ROAD
                    COLUMBUS, OHIO  43212
                    APARTMENT # 123

                    (614)443-7785
```

EXPERIENCE:

August 1975 –
Present

CERO'S AND KLINES'
Canton, Ohio

Assistant to the Store Manager/Merchandising Hardlines

Redesigned departments including: redefining of classifications, merchandise, and fixture presentations resulting in sales increases of 10-20%.
Coordinated the efforts of buyers and display department personnel to achieve aesthetically pleasing, cohesive vignettes representing market trends and store direction.
Created more awareness of merchandise presentation and coordination throughout the home furnishings divisions.

June 1973–
July 1975

HOUSE FURNISHINGS, INC.

Buyer/Merchandiser/Coordinator: Accessories

Reduced the resource selection by 60% and increased volume by 15% while opening 50% fewer stores.
Raised the net profitability of department by 35%.
Raised the turnover rate of merchandise in stores from 1.5 to 2.5 times per year via tighter selections, controls and the implementation of an inventory control system.
Within capacity of merchandising consultant to over 250 stores in the area of gifts and accessories, have shopped all major national accessory markets and researched, coordinated and published 5 service manuals which are utilized for resources, merchandise and display techniques.
Directed dealers with designing, merchandising and displaying their in-store gift shops.

(Continued)

January 1970-
June 1973

SUNSHINE DEPARTMENT STORE
224 West Market Street.
Cleveland, Ohio

Department Manager: Men's Accessories, Candy, Smoke Shop

Reduced personnel budget by 30-man-hours per week through
more efficient use of personnel.
Supervised 25 employees.
Reordered all merchandise sold in departments.
Responsible for all department areas including personnel,
housekeeping, displays, merchandising.

EDUCATION: B.S. Business Management
Bowling Green University

References on request

GEORGE W. WILLIAMS
244 Washington Boulevard
Flushing, New York 11304
212-492-6490

OBJECTIVE

To obtain position in supervisory capacity with Metallurgical Laboratory.

EXPERIENCE

1/75-Date

Technical Advisor and Editor, Scientific Journal of America, New York, N.Y. Write and edit articles on latest developments and innovations in ferrous industries; conduct in-field research for collection of data for feature articles; public relations responsibilities with domestic industries related to metallurgical processes.

5/72-1/75

Production Supervisor, Metallurgical Division, CITOR Chemical Laboratories, White Plains, N.Y. Conducted quality control checks on Chemical, Physical Metallurgy, Metallography regarding future production requirements; handled customer complaints with respect to both metallurgical and non-metallurgical process deviations; ordered all supplies necessary to heat treating; supervised and scheduled assignments of laboratory technicians and production workers.

8/67-5/70

Metallurgical Trainee, Allison Steel Works, Pittsburgh, Pa. Trained in metallurgical aspects of metal defect reduction, non-destructive testing, chemical analysis development and implementation of processes involving physical testing, cost reduction; gained experience in Quality Control, including statistics control charts, and developed skills in both metallurgical and non-metallurgical process deviations. Assisted in supervision of eight laboratory technicians.

EDUCATION

B.S. in Metallurgical Engineering, June, 1967, Wheeling University, Pennsylvania.

PROFESSIONAL SOCIETIES

Member of American Society of Mining Engineers, American Metallurgist Society, Institute of Metallurgical Engineering.

REFERENCES

Furnished on request.

NIKITA WYCKOFF
2011 Connecticut Road
Island Park, NY 11558
516-889-0448

RESUME CAPSULE:Worked as Mutual Fund Accountant for
twenty years in variety of corporations, also included thirteen
years' experience in bookkeeping.

EXPERIENCE

1983-present   Mutual Fund Accountant, Capital Advisory Service, Inc., New York City. Pre-
                pared monthly financial statements; calculated net asset value of Fund's capital
                stock; maintained full set of books, including general ledger; recorded daily
                transactions and assigned data for computer processing, calculated interest on
                bonds and short-term paper.

1982–1983   Mutual Fund Accountant, Walker's Management, Inc., New York City. Respon-
                sibilities same as above.

1979–1982   Mutual Fund Accountant, J.R. Stern Advisors and Distributors, New York.
                Worked on financial statements, general ledger, S.E.C. reports (N-IR and N-IQ),
                taxes.

1965–1979   Mutual Fund Accountant and Bookkeeper, Brewster Management Corporation,
                Long Island. Complete responsibility for maintaining Fund's books, including
                general ledger, pricing of Fund's shares, supervision of clerical staff of four,
                liaison with Custodian and Transfer Agent, general correspondence and all
                duties connected with conducting the Fund's business transactions.

EDUCATION

LL.B. of the University of Riga, Latvia, Faculty of Law and Economics, 1965.

Certificate in Investment Analysis, 1970, Finance Institute of New York.

LANGUAGES

Fluency in Russian, Latvian, French, German.

REFERENCES: On request.

Joanne Mitchell
36 Riggs Street
Cedar Rapids, Iowa 52465
(319) 958-9362

Job Objective

Private Nurse

Experience

6/75-present
Nurse, St. Johns Hospital, Cedar Rapids, Iowa
Responsible for general care of patients in
cardiac division: took histories, kept charts,
administered medication, prepared patients for
tests and treatments.

Nurse, Cedar Rapids Hospital, Cedar Rapids, Iowa
As a staff nurse on surgical floor, duties
consisted of preparing patients for operation and
treatment, administering medication (kept complete records of all narcotics), assisting in
physical therapy and attending personal needs of
patients.

Education

1972-1975
B.S. in Nursing, Iowa State College, Boise, Iowa

References

On request

MARVIN MILTON
24 Woodbine Drive
Cherry Hill, N.J. 08003
(609) 685-4039

EXPERIENCE

1981-present

<u>Customer Relations Manager</u>, Premium Publishing Company,
Morris Hills, N.J. Manage Customer Relations Dept.,
with staff of 13 full-time employees. Maintain effective
and efficient customer relations, maintain and control
procedure of work flow, act as liaison between sales,
operations, and customers. Analyze and make decisions
for adjustments, credits and debits. Involved in all
phases including processing of orders, shipping, returns,
sales, credits. Prepare reports (weekly and monthly) on
statistics, problems, and make recommendations when needed.
Handle all problems related to personnel, vacations, time
cards, interviewing, hiring and training.

1975-1981

<u>Administrator-Office Manager</u>, Civic Center, Plainfield,
N.J. Maintained and supervised bookkeeping and accounting
records according to established practice. A/P, A/R,
payroll, purchasing, check reconciliation, general ledger.
Prepared periodic financial statements, reviewed budget,
maintained accurate membership records; handled enrollment
of new members; prepared calendar of events for all
affiliated groups, coordinated the use of facilities;
supervised building and maintenance staff. Administered
and executed all policies made by executive board.

1970-1974

<u>Field Sales Representative</u>, Martin's Gift Shop, Avenue of
the Americas, New York. Called on wholesalers, chain and
retail stores as representative of manufacturer and
importer of novelties, souvenirs, costume jewelry, etc.
Involved extensive travel throughout midwest states. Set
up and exhibited at numerous trade shows.

EDUCATION

1970

Dearborn Jr. College, Ridgelake, Colorado.
Two-year certificate, Business Administration.

1975-1977

Bradley Business School, Rutherford, N.J.
Night courses in Business Administration.

<u>References</u>

Available upon request

Washington J. Brooks
2341 Harrison Avenue
Houston, Texas 77003

(713) 651-9812

Job Objective: Duplicating Specialist—Photo and Printing

Experience

1978–1989   Skilled Duplicating Operator
United Oil Company, Houston, Texas

Operated and maintained offset duplicating machines to reproduce
black and white or color copies from metal or paper masters.
Equipment varied from 1250-multilith, 2650-multilith automatic, to
Davidson 400 and 600.

Operated photostat camera to produce prints of varying sizes. Prepared
negatives (stripping) for plate-making in black and white and multicolor work. Mixed chemicals needed for photographic process. Prepared
black and white slides, ozalids, operated offset cameras, and handled
some half-tone offset photography.

1975–1978   Duplicating Trainee
Texarco Duplicating Services, Houston, Texas

Acquired a working knowledge of photography, stripping and plate-
making. Operated automatic feed and manual offset duplicating
machines to produce black and white copies from paper masters. Met
established standards for producing high quality copies. Made adjustments for proper ink flow, inked machine, adjusted water rollers, set
up machine for various types of paper and positioned master as
necessary.

Education   Willow Grove High School, Diploma 1974

References   On request.

Martha Bender
1600 Nevada Street, N.W.
Washington, D.C. 20006
(202) 929-3006
(202) 787-3400

GOAL: Seeking a challenging position as a Senior-Level Legal
Assistant which provides an opportunity for both greater
responsibilities and future advancement.

EXPERIENCE:

October 1984   Morris, Banker, & Rand
to Present   15 State Street
                Washington, D.C.

CORPORATE PARALEGAL: Responsibilities include training and
supervising Unit Trust Department Legal Assistants in the
preparation of materials for the issuance and sale of Fortune
100 Corporate and Municipal Bond Funds, compliance with
relevant SEC and NASD fund regulations (including 1933 and
1940 Act requirements), direction of financial printing,
and coordination of closings with key sponsors (Smith Barney,
Kidder Peabody, Drexel Burnham) and evaluation services
(Moody's, Standard and Poors). Also assist in preparation
of other corporate closings including mergers, debt
restructuring, reorganization of Limited Partnerships, and
stock offerings.

January 1983 to   Estate of Harris Co., Bankruptcy
October 1984   14 Wall Street
                   New York, N.Y.

REAL ESTATE PARALEGAL: Responsibilities included reconciliation of Real Estate Claims against the Estate, recording
monthly progress of claims processing, and discounting leases
to determine fair rental value of breach of lease claims.
Developed and maintained a series of indexed systems for internal
and court-ordered changes and final disposition of these claims.
Also assisted in the development and implementation of EDP
System to record this information for all claims against the
Estate.

EDUCATION: New York University, New York, N.Y.
              Took several graduate-level courses in Psychology.

              Skidmore College, Saratoga, N.Y.
              B.A. English, Minor: Fine Arts
              HONORS: Dean's List, 1980-82
              ACTIVITIES: Publicity Director for Student Program Board,
              Activities coordinator for Seminar in Communications, Student
              Council, Editor of Literary Magazine.

REFERENCES: Furnished upon request.

ADAM STERN

100 Sycamore Lane
Nashville, Tenn. 37204
(615) 595-1309 (home)

(615) 586-7000 (work)

OBJECTIVE:

Experienced holder of ABA-approved trusts and estates paralegal certificate seeks challenging position.

EXPERIENCE:

1984 - Present

Elliot, Elliot & Farber, Nashville, Tenn.
Trusts and Estates Settlement Assistant.
Prepare, analyze and compile data of new estates; transfer securities, brokerage, custody and check accounts for estates and trusts; terminate and distribute assets of accounts; compile and prepare financial statements, fiduciary and personal tax returns; pay estate and trust expenses for new and ongoing accounts; research and interpret pertinent information concerning estates and trusts, court experience.

1983

Burton Advertising Associates, Inc., Nashville, Tenn.
Assistant to Bookkeeper.
Pressured job, involving deadlines, heavy workload, computing payroll for 250 workers weekly from 3 offices, programming mag card, billing and checking balance sheet for taxes paid by employees.

1982

Carnegie Records, Nashville, Tenn.
Administrative Assistant in the Public Relations Department.
Worked with confidential material and gained familiarity with office procedures.

1978-80

Acme's Emporium, Nashville, Tenn.
Clerk.
Worked to finance education while attending classes on a full-time basis. Successfully assumed the responsibilities of cashier, sales and opening and closing of department.

1977-78

IBM, Endicott, Tenn.
Co-op Assistant.
Duties included terminal work, typing, filing, and heavy phone contact.

EDUCATION:

University of Tennessee, Nashville, Tenn.
Lawyers Assistant Program.
Specialization in Trusts and Estates. (ABA approved) December 1983

Richmond College, Richmond, Va.
Bachelor of Arts, Sociology, May 1983
Pertinent Course Work: Accounting 1, Statistics, BASIC computer, SPSS Computer.

REFERENCES:

Furnished upon request.

JAMES MICHAEL SOLOMON

1619 Lexington Avenue, Apt. 19B
New York, New York 10128
Home: (212) 369-2751
Work: (212) 940-7721

JOB OBJECTIVE:

A supervisory position offering increasing responsibility in the area of
law firm administration.

RELEVANT WORK
EXPERIENCE:

January 1984   Paralegal/Case Supervisor. Smith, Collins, Frederick,
to Present   Clarkson & Cohen, New York, New York. Handle ad-
                ministrative responsibilities including hiring permanent
                and temporary paralegals, distributing and supervising work,
                and working in conjunction with other departments such as
                word processing; prepare billing to clients, communicate
                with clients, digest depositions, legal research, create
                trial exhibits, and organize antitrust litigation files
                specifically organizing, categorizing, and cataloging
                large document productions.

Summers   Work experience includes clerking at various retail
1979-1983   establishments (including Montgomery Ward) and a bank;
                responsibilities included sales, administrative, and
                office work and collections.

EDUCATION: New York University, New York, New York
                School of Continuing Education.
                Courses completed include Practical Account Management
                (emphasis on planning, workflow, research, presentations,
                and client relations); Filmmaking: Techniques and Tech-
                nology; and Film Production I.

                Adelphi University, Garden City, New York
                Completed lawyer's assistant program (ABA-approved) in
                winter of 1983; instruction included drafting and com-
                municative legal techniques and legal research.

                Boston University, Boston, Massachusetts
                Graduated June 1982, with Bachelor of Arts Degree;
                Major - English; Minor - Psychology. Courses include
                Public Speaking, Techniques of Debating, Newswriting and
                Reporting, and Photography (journalism).

                Extracurricular Activities: Program director and disc jockey
                at WTBU (university radio station); administration, organiza-
                tion and planning in connection with presidential election
                campaign; and personal solicitation of funds for various
                charities.

REFERENCES: Furnished upon request.

Stanley Y. Gerbreem
12 Central Street, South
Omaha, Nebraska 68114
(402) 456-0976

Job Goal: Payroll Supervisor

Experience

1971 - present   Vanderbilt, Lowe and Thomas, Inc., Omaha, Nebraska
Payroll Clerk

While in training, became familiar with corporate personnel
and payroll policies, various unit payroll practices, benefit
plan program, and appropriate tax manuals.

Examine and process changes to the basic computerized payroll
file for approximately 500 employees. Maintain control totals
for different types of changes by unit (increases, new hires,
terminations). Examine time sheets and other records to
apply overtime and exception pay practices, processing special
payments (sales bonus, incentive awards); and prepare manual
checks for emergency situations.

Maintain employee absence and vacation records. Compose
routine correspondence. Solve discrepancy problems.

1969 - 1971   Meyers & Harris Distribution Center, Omaha, Nebraska
Clerk in Marketing Research Department

Performed standardized clerical tasks following company
procedures. Maintained salary ledger for department,
assembled and classified vouchers, entered postings for
the department budgets.

Education   Portland District High School, Portland, Oregon
Diploma of Business Studies, 1967

Military   Served a two-year term in the Coast Guard.

References   Available on request.

Barbara Winters
1645 West Brook Drive
Passaic, New Jersey 07056
(201) 455-6767

EMPLOYMENT
HISTORY:

WAVERLY CORPORATION (PULP AND PAPER COMPANY), 3722 Boston Post Road, New Rochelle, New York

7/2/73 -
Present

Administer Corporate Savings and Investment Plan, Retirement Plan and Long Term Disability Plan.

SAVINGS AND INVESTMENT PLAN

Maintain all records of activity. Review and approve new enrollments and terminations. Calculate and process monthly cash transactions connected with transfer of company and employee funds to the Trustee. Prepare information to Corporate Tax Department in connection with various S.E.C. reports. Assist and advise local Benefits Representatives with administration of the Plan.

RETIREMENT PLAN

Calculate and file with actuaries refunds of contributions on all salaried non-vested terminations. Deposit and refund cash contributions received from foreign and domestic subsidiaries. Act as trouble shooter between hourly locations and actuaries.

DISABILITY PLAN

Calculate monthly Long Term Disability premiums. Coordinate and process salaried Long Term Disability and New York State Disability claims. Maintain all records and correspondence.

11/27/72 -
6/29/73

TRENTON MEMORIAL HOSPITAL, 2167 Arbor Avenue, Trenton, New Jersey
(Unemployment Insurance Clerk)

Administered unemployment insurance claims.

(Continued)

4/8/68 -   CLAYTON INDUSTRIES, 6767 Williamsburg Avenue, Trenton, New
  11/22/72   Jersey
                (Personnel Assistant)

                Recruited and oriented clerical, production and some technical
                personnel. Processed merit and cost of living increases.
                Administered Blue Cross, Major Medical, Life Insurance, Work-
                men's Compensation, New York State Disability, Unemployment
                Insurance, etc.

2/14/66 -   WESTBURY INC., 23 West Canal Street, New York, New York
  4/5/68   (Assistant Personnel Supervisor)

                Recruited, oriented clerical employees. Processed performance
                appraisals and merit increases. Maintained employee records.

EDUCATION: Villanova University, B.B.A., 1966.

References available on request.

JEANETTE ELWELL
32-22 224th Street
Brooklyn, New York 11263
212-962-2668

JOB OBJECTIVE: To apply experience, mature insight, and education
                 to position in personnel administration where
                 effective personnel management can be promoted.

EXPERIENCE PERTINENT TO OBJECTIVE

1981-present   Personnel Manager, Hart and Dunlap Co., Inc., New York City.
               Reported to Vice President of Personnel in this major publishing
               firm in fulfilling responsibilities as supervisor of personnel
               services for New York office. Conducted salary surveys,
               established salary ranges and progression rates for each level.
               Installed and maintained job evaluation plans, questionnaires,
               application forms, etc. Revised and formulated training programs,
               designed progress reports and initiated appraisal procedures for
               employee performance. Ran successful recruiting campaigns for
               new employees for reference book subsidiary. Initiated and
               implemented programs to improve and utilize potential of staff
               members. Represented company at hearings with City and State
               Boards. Was involved in development of company policies with
               responsibility for interpretation with implementation in every-
               day practice. Consulted with managers on numerous problems such
               as manpower planning, upgrading, performance evaluation.

EDUCATION

M.B.A., Management - Graduate School of Business Administration, New York
University, New York, New York, June 1981.

B.A., History, Rochester University, New York, February 1979.

Personnel Management Course, National Conference Board of Industrial Management,
1980. Techniques and planning for effective personnel programs were developed
with the use of group case histories and lectures.

REFERENCES

Upon request.

STELLA DAVIDOFF
165 Williams Street
Dallas, Texas 75213
(818) 929-3456
(816) 921-4000

OBJECTIVE

To obtain a position within an organization that will provide continued growth, learning, and opportunity to contribute as a Human Resource Professional.

RELATED EXPERIENCE

4/88–Present *Client/Personal Representative*,
Career Blazers, Dallas, Texas
- National temporary placement service.
- Enhance delivery of service to established accounts; prospect and develop new accounts. Cater to the individual needs of client companies.
- Ensure customer satisfaction by backing promises with strict attention to administrative details. Match temporary employee to the job requirements.
- Recruit temporary managers, accountants, secretaries, word processing specialists, and other clerical personnel at college campuses, professional organizations, etc. for client corporations.
- Conduct 30 to 50 exempt/nonexempt applicant screenings and interviews weekly.
- Follow-up sales staff contacts of new and established clients.

1979–1987 *Assistant to Director/Head Music Counselor*,
Moore County Day School, Dallas, Texas
- Conducted informational tours for prospective campers and their families.
- Projected and promoted Hillel School's image; set a high performance pace.
- Supervised team responsible for preparing camp for openings/closings each year.
- Planned and prepared schedule of activities for each group and counselor.
- Supervised all music and music-related activities.
- Produced and Directed several large scale performances throughout the season.

1981–1987 *Vocal Music Teacher*,
Public Schools, Dallas, Texas
- Taught vocal music to individual and groups of students; emphasized musical, social, and scholastic development.
- Planned curriculum to enhance students' learning, growth, and self-esteem.
- Took into account students' abilities and potentials.
- Achieved excellent results with "reluctant and eager" learners.

EDUCATION

June 1989, Expected Graduation, M.B.A. Degree in
Industrial/Organizational Psychology
University of Texas

1985 B.A. Degree in Psychology, Minor in Personnel Management
Baylor University

BARBARA JO BERNSTEIN
307 East 78th St.
New York, NY 10021
(212) 429-5467

OBJECTIVE

A position in personnel with a salary commensurate with the opportunities afforded.

WORK EXPERIENCE

6/83 to present

Hapcourt Research Company, Inc., 789 Park Avenue, N.Y.C.

Personnel Interviewer

Responsible for all non-exempt and some exempt recruitment for the parent company and several subsidiaries (approximately 1,800 employees).

Counseling duties included employee-subsidiary relations and formal exit interviews.

Involved in special reports dealing with EEO, Affirmative Action programs, Wage and Salary surveys, and employee computerized programs.

Responsible for handling medical and dental benefits for The Psychological Corporation, a subsidiary of 250 employees.

Administrative Assistant

Primary responsibility was to obtain permission to reprint material in our school textbooks; also responsible for some secretarial work.

9/82 to 4/83

E.F. Hutton, 280 Park Avenue, N.Y.C.

Secretary

Responsible for all secretarial duties for an account executive.

EDUCATION

Muhlenberg College, B.A. History, June 1982. Penn State. Instructor's Level I certification in secondary history education. Graduated with a cumulative average of 3.15.

Katherine Gibbs, Certificate of Completion ENTREE program, August 1982.

New York University Graduate School of Business Administration, Currently attending evenings, January 1985 to present.

REFERENCES:

On request.

Dorothy Rogers
145 Pacific Drive, Apt. 2C
Marine del Ray, CA   90087
(213) 346-6144

Experience   1970-present
                  Photographer, Wilson Studio, Malibu, CA.
                  Chief photographer in still-life, high
                  fashion studio. Taking pictures, directing
                  models, booking locations...black and white,
                  4 colors.

                  1960-1970
                  Beauty Fashion Photographer. Trend Magazine,
                  New York City, N.Y. Developed analytical
                  themes for feature articles, news stories,
                  and photo essays. Hired and booked models,
                  responsible for stylists.

                  1958-1961
                  Free-lance Photographer

Exhibits   1971
                  Famous Woman, Fine Arts Center, Los Angeles,
                  CA.

                  1966
                  In Black and White, Beveridge Bldg., Chicago,
                  Ill.

Education   Ellison School of Photography, Ellison, Ca.,
                  1960
                  High School of Music and Art, New York City,
                  N.Y., 1958

References on request

C. KIMBALL PRETTSON

14 Panther Place
Stamford, Connecticut 06814

Telephone
Days—(203) 674-0867
Eves.—(203) 976-3457

Capabilities:
The ability to work independently and creatively with the maturity necessary to complete high-pressure jobs correctly and on time.

Present Employment:
1976–present
Production Manager for Meridian Studios
Port Chester, NY
Meridian is a full service house specializing in large format photography for advertising, slide production, and art work. Meridian services many of the major corporations and agencies in Westchester and Fairfield Counties.

Responsibilities:
- Head up and oversee all in-house production.
- Control job flow and client specifics.

Prior Experience:
1973–1976
Chief Assistant to George Taubert, Taubert Studios, Mount Vernon, New York

1971–1973
Owned and ran with partner a commerical studio.

1970-1971
Head of black and white commerical lab.

Professional Education:
Germain School of Photography 1968–1970

Familiar Formats:
Five years extensive 4×5 and 8×10 view plus all small mm. formats.

Job Assignments:
- 4 × 5 and 8 × 10 product photography
- Catalog Shootings
- 2¼ sq.—ad promotion—corporate and college
- 4 × 5 and 35mm. flat art
- 35 mm. Kodalith slides, negative and positive, hand dyed and jelled
- 35 mm. Diazo slides
- Vu Graphs—Multiple overlays
- Mounting and packaging

Darkroom Experience:
Complete black and white capabilities

References:
Available upon request.

Helen Roland
46 Robinwood Drive
Toledo, Ohio 43612

Home phone: 419-236-3715

Employment experience
<u>Employment experience</u>

1977-present   Mary Magdalene Hospital
                             45 Parson Street
                             Toledo, Ohio
                             <u>Physical Therapist--Children's
                             Ward</u>. Post-operative and long-term
                             therapy with preadolescents.
                             Initiated prosthetic acclimatization
                             program which was adapted for adults.

1972-1977   Perkins University Hospital
                             Maybury Road
                             Toledo, Ohio
                             <u>Part-Time Physical Therapist</u>
                             This was in conjunction with a degree
                             program. Worked with geriatric and
                             juvenile patients.

<u>Education:</u>

1977   Physical Therapist Certification
                             Perkins University

1972   B.A. Wisconsin University
                             Major: Biology.   Minor: Psychology

                             REFERENCES ON REQUEST

Thomas Egan
52 Elm Street
Harrison, New York 10502

Home Telephone: 914-682-4576   Office Telephone: 914-682-1000, ext. 211

WORK EXPERIENCE:

        1976-present   **Harrison Police Force**, Harrison, New York
                              After four years on force, was promoted to
                              sergeant in charge of the juvenile division.
                              In 1986 was promoted to captain and police
                              chief.

        1974-1976   **Patrolman**, New Jersey State Police
                              Morristown Barracks

EDUCATION:

New Jersey State Police Academy at Morristown, 1974
B.A., Lafayette College, Easton, Pennsylvania, 1972

CLUB MEMBERSHIPS, AFFILIATIONS:

        1985-Present: Chairman, Westchester Big Brothers of America
        1978-1979:   Secretary Treasurer Patrolman's Benevolent
                            Association
        1980-1982:   Coordination, Police Athletic League

REFERENCES: On request

ERNEST COHEN
16 Denver Lane
Denver, CO 80202

(725) 842-9863
(725) 644-7600

SUMMARY

Production Manager with creative abilities in concept design, client relations, operations and logistics planning, financial and inventory control and promotion.

ADMINISTRATIVE ACCOMPLISHMENTS

- Established accounts payable/accounts receivable systems to meet the needs of three different businesses, including the calculation and distribution of commission checks.

- Reviewed and evaluated prices for office equipment and supplies, interviewing and developing relationships with wholesalers and retailers to reduce purchasing costs.

- Coordinated and controlled the transportation of hundreds of props varying in size and value, arranging for safe delivery and insurance coverage.

- Improved distribution of promotional material to over 500 clients monthly, utilizing a computerized mailing list and supervisory skills to simplify the process.

- Arranged for catering of meals for production staffs of up to 50 people, evaluating menu preferences, checking visual attractiveness, and supervising delivery of services in a variety of indoor and outdoor locations.

CREATIVE/CONSULTING SKILLS

- Develop rapport with clients, utilizing active listening skills to ensure a mutual understanding of the desired concept for development.

- Offer clients several options for achieving the style they seek, combining my ability to think creatively and apply the perspective of my professional experience.

WORK HISTORY

10/86—Present *Freelance Photo Stylist*

Major clients: Black & Decker, Lorus, Ralph Lauren, Revlon, Robert Peritz Designer, Timex, John Wiley, and Warner Bros.

10/84—10/86 *Central Office Manager/Production Coordinator/Full Charge Bookkeeper*

Paul Christensen Photography Studio & Ted Morrison Photography Studio, New York City.

9/83—10/84 *Purchasing Agent*
Yonkers General Hospital

SPECIAL SKILLS

IBM XT 286—Lotus 1-2-3, Volkswriter, Q & A Word Processing, Managing your Money.

EDUCATION

— Boulder College, Denver, CO

B.A., Psychology, Awarded June 1983

Dean's List

— Assisted Fulbright Scholar in the production of a documentary aired on cable television: "Out of the Double Bind: A View of Bilingual Education"

Business and personal references upon request.

ELLA TURNER   212-822-9416
4820 Bronx Road
Bronx, New York 10467

EXPERIENCE

July 1973-Present   Production Manager, Publications, Inc., New York City.
                     Serve as liaison between the Editorial and Sales
                     Departments. Responsibilities include the overall
                     preparation and layout of two major trade publications,
                     including annual directories. Design and makeup of ads
                     and reprints, complete follow through of advertising
                     materials, insertion orders and advertisement schedules.
                     Direct contact and working knowledge of printing
                     schedules and full responsibility of and for printing/
                     production costs.

December 1972-   Assistant to the Coordinator, United Society of Magazine
November 1973   Photographers, New York City. Entire processing of ap-
                     plicants and potential members; presenting their work
                     to Board of Trustees for final acceptance to the Society.

July 1971-   Sales Secretary, Media Management, New York City. Handled
November 1972   secretarial duties and expansion into overall partici-
                     pation in circulation and production responsibilities.
                     Varied functions in this position included proofreading,
                     handling of insertion orders, contracts, advertising
                     material and billing.

EDUCATION

Academic Degree from St. Anthony High School - June 1971.

REFERENCES

Will be furnished upon request.

MARGARET YORK

620 North Illinois Street   Arlington, Virginia 22205   (202) 847-6721
(703) 874-1000

SUMMARY: Applications specialist with the following experience:

- Skilled in PL/1, FORTRAN, BASIC, JCL, OS Utilities, MODEL 204 DBMS, XEROX 9700 Printing System, Assembler concepts, COBOL reading, structured methods, top-down design and development, speaking, writing, teaching.

- Supervised 1-3 programmers.

- Designed and programmed DBMS application of 300 modules.

- Made customer site studies and wrote study reports.

- Developed high-throughput utility for authors to type own texts and receive computer-printed formatted manuscripts.

- Worked in application areas: Federal Budget, Scientific Programming, Administrative Systems.

EDUCATION: BA Long Island University, New York 1967
Mathematics major

EXPERIENCE: PROGRAMMER/ANALYST. Dept. of the Interior, Washington, D.C.

1976 -   Designed and programmed Database Systems relating the
present   federal budget, laws, Congressional committees; user-friendly, table-driven. Supervised junior programmers for several years. Analyzed legislative information process; wrote study reports of legislative clerk offices. Devised and programmed utility for authors to type papers into TSO/SPF and receive formatted manuscripts printed on the XEROX 9700.

6/67-9/76   ASSOCIATE PROGRAMMER. UNIVAC, Allentown, Pennsylvania
Wrote compiler modules. Wrote and converted aerospace programs. Wrote and installed time accounting programs. Used automated module library system. Wrote programming production library plan. Wrote MIS user manuals. Worked on suggestion processing system.

REFERENCES: On Request

Willing to relocate

Maria T. Gonzales
560 Attala Drive
Bakersfield, California 93309

(805) 651-3987

Job Objective: Programmer Trainee

Experience

1989-present   Atlas Electronics - Bakersfield, California
                    Computer Operator

                    Operates and monitors digital computer equipment
                    (370-155 and 360-65). Follows established programs
                    and new programs under development. Selects
                    appropriate processing devices (card, tape, disc)
                    and loads computer. Observes lights on console and
                    storage devices to report deviations from standards.

                    Maintains records of job performance; checks and main-
                    tains controls on each job. Solves operational
                    problems and checks out new programs; assists in
                    making necessary corrections. Assists less experienced
                    operators.

1987-1989   Bee Newspaper - Modesto, California
                    Bookkeeper/Clerk Typist

                    Typed invoices, posted and maintained records and files;
                    made and verified computations. Typed classified ads
                    and sent to composing department.

Education   1987 B.S. degree from University of California
                    Mathematics Major - Business studies and computer training
                    Activities - Advertising Manager of campus newspaper
                                 Volunteer hospital work

References   Provided on request.

FRANK BEATTY
50 Union Boulevard
Union City, N.J.   07087
201-864-4239

OBJECTIVE: Position with State agency of investigative and
             correctional nature on larger scale than that
             of previous experience.

EXPERIENCE

1971-Date   Caseworker - Investigator, Union City Dept. of
                 Social Services. Investigate eligibility and
                 maintain clients on public welfare.

1966-1971   Parole Officer, Narcotics Division, New Jersey
                 Narcotic Addiction Control Center. Conducted
                 investigations, supervised narcotic addicts,
                 apprehended violators.

EDUCATION

M.B.A., Public Administration, February 1970, Fairleigh
School of Business Administration, Upton University, N.J.

B.B.A., February 1966, Fairleigh School of Business Administration, Upton University, N.J.

HONORS

William Bucknell Scholarship Award
John Fairleigh Scholarship Award
Psi Chi Honorary Professional Psychology Fraternity

REFERENCES

Suitable personal references furnished upon request.

Claudia Johnson
16 Quincy Court
Silver Springs, MD 72415
(208) 541-2246

OBJECTIVE: A public relations position managing publications, publicity, and special events.

PROFESSIONAL EXPERIENCE:

5/84–12/88 **SILVER SPRINGS CENTER**
Communications Consultant: created new logo; restructured format and focus of monthly publication; wrote and edited first issue of revised publication; negotiated with and coordinated printers, typesetters and graphic artists, and redesigned stationery and monthly direct mail item.

8/82–10/83 **MARYLAND COLLEGE OF OPTOMETRY**
Public Relations Associate: edited and produced three quarterly newsletters; wrote and placed news releases; arranged television and radio interviews; conducted bi-monthly Continuing Education seminars; interfaced with the media during press conferences and special events, and created visual information displays.

3/82–5/82 **WASHINGTON STAR**
Reporter: researched and interviewed for information and wrote news and feature articles.

5/81–9/81 *Freelance Writer:* wrote feature for health organization and product publicity for advertising agency.

1/78–8/80 **REGENT INTERNATIONAL SCHOOL**
Teacher: taught third- and fourth-grade classes in multi-lingual school; supervised five aides and student-teacher; designed specialized programs and record-keeping systems, and produced and co-directed musical which involved over sixty children.

EDUCATION:

9/81–5/82 **NEW YORK SCHOOL OF ADVERTISING AND JOURNALISM**
Diploma in Advertising and Certificate of Journalism.

9/72–5/77 **VASSAR COLLEGE**, Poughkeepsie, NY. Bachelor of Arts-English.

9/74–5/75 **PACE UNIVERSITY**, Briarcliffe, NY. Junior Year Exchange Program.

HONORS:

5/82 **THE SULLIVAN MEMORIAL AWARD**: for student work in writing and preparation of company publications, presented by the International Association of Business Communicators.

References and portfolio available on request.

CONFIDENTIAL

HELEN C. CHESTERFIELD
43 Crescent Lane
Port Washington, NY 11050
(516) 384-9227

SUMMARY: Ten years' public relations and advertising experience in multi-division corporation and public relations firms. Direct experience included financial and
product publicity; business and technical articles and speeches; institutional
and product public relations and advertising; shareholder and employee relations. Supervised department and directed successful efforts of public relations
and advertising agencies.

EXPERIENCE:

Nov. 1983   **Director of Communications**
to present   **GAF, Inc.,** Woodside, NY

Advertising, public relations, shareholder relations for this American Stock
Exchange company.

March 1981   **Account Executive**
to Sept. 1983   **Howard P. Schmidt Associates,** New York, NY

Corporate, financial and product public relations for industrial, consumer and
financial services companies. Corporate planning, executive speeches, annual
reports, brochures, feature articles, news releases and scripts. Also analyst
meetings, press conferences, marketing seminars, broadcast interviews, corporate advertising. Good relations with all segments of financial community, and
trade, general and business media.

April 1979   **Account Executive**
to Feb. 1981   **Spahr, Smith and Associates,** New York, NY

Supervised corporate and financial public relations activities for client firms
(construction, medical products, leisure time, electronics). Wrote and placed
news releases, speeches, feature articles, annual reports, brochures and leaflets.
Arranged for press conferences, analyst meetings, and personal interviews.

May 1970   **Advertising and Public Relations Manager**
to March 1979   **Page Co., Inc.,** New York, NY

Coordinated all internal and external (agency) advertising and public relations
activities, scheduled space advertising and product publicity, prepared advertising budgets and analyses. Also originated sales literature, directed mail,
organized trade shows, edited sales newsletter and house organ, prepared
annual reports, and supervised staff of four.

EDUCATION: B.S., New York University (1969)
Undergraduate, University of Chicago

MEMBERSHIP: American Public Relations Society
New York Public Relations Association

REFERENCES: Available upon request

JOANNA CURTIS
29 East 12th Street
New York, New York 10003
212-669-7839

JOB OBJECTIVE   Seeking position as public relations consultant.

EXPERIENCE

1971-present   Legal Secretary, S. Jerome Berg Associates,
                     Bronx, New York. Handle legal correspondence,
                     great deal of technical, legal details requiring
                     knowledge of legal terms and format, much
                     telephone contact with clients, appointment
                     scheduling, often working under pressure to
                     meet court dates, etc. so that necessary
                     documents are completed on time.

1968-1971   French Teacher, Brookville High School, N.Y.

1967-1968   French Translator, Markum Engineering Corp.,
                     New York. Translated correspondence and reports
                     from branch office in Paris. Acted as inter-
                     preter in Public Relations Department and liaison
                     between French engineers and New York office staff.

1965-1967   French Teacher, Strauss High School, New York.

EDUCATION

M.A., 1967, French - Middlebury College, Vermont
B.A., 1965, French - Middlebury College, Vermont

SPECIAL SKILLS

Fluency in French, Spanish, German
Stenotype Machine
Writing and Editing

REFERENCES

Furnished upon request.

Gail R. Geltzer
310 West 30th Street
New York, New York 10001
(212) 694-0074

St. Vincent's Hospital—Assitant Director of Public Information
1979–present

Describe, interpret, promote and publicize policies, patient care services, medical research, medical, nursing, and paraprofessional education programs of this hospital to its various publics to earn their understanding, support and acceptance. (Publics include patients, contributors, staff, faculty and students, trustees, volunteers, other agencies, general and local community.) As editor of an award-winning internal-external house organ, develop ideas, do bulk of writing, total layout, and production of five-times-a-year, 16,000 circulation publication. Responsibilities include heavy press liaison with science, and hospital reporters on daily papers, television and radio stations, news, medical, health, and hospital magazines, government press officers, freelance writers, educational film producers. Write releases, arrange press conferences. Extensive liaison with public relations officers of affiliated institutions, other health and welfare agencies, city, state, and federal health agencies, etc. in joint efforts, exchange of information. Give public relations' counsel, editorial help to professional staff. Work with hospital's development office on fund-raising events.

The Salvation Army—Public Information Associate
1970–1979

Planned, wrote, produced major publications interpreting this noted agency's program of family counseling, social action and welfare research to a variety of publics: annual report, a monthly bulletin to contributors, internal staff house organ, bimonthly newsletter for board and committee members, fund-raising campaign literature, brochures. Wrote radio and television spots, speeches as needed. Wrote and/or placed news and feature stories ranging from pilot demonstration study results to appraisals of legislation in fields of health, housing, aging, family and child welfare, narcotics addiction, courts, etc. Wrote case stories for *Times* Neediest Cases, of which agency was a major beneficiary. Job required keeping abreast of entire social welfare field and being able to translate into lay language, technical, often complicated concepts of caseworks, medicine, psychiatry, community organization and legalities.

The American Nursing Association—Publication and Public Relations Consultant
1967–1970

Disseminated information about ANA's Department of Hospital Nursing to membership, allied professional groups (American Health Care Association, etc.) and public through articles, books, brochures, press releases and promotional materials. Planned, wrote, produced pamphlets, newsletters, including national newsletter for psychiatric aids and technicians funded by a pharmaceutical company.

American Paramedical Association—Director of Public Information
1966–1970

Directed recruitment program for occupational therapists under grant from National Foundation. Created recruitment literature, supervised distribution nationally to prospective students, universities, guidance counselors, hospital and medical groups assisting with recruitment. Worked with newspapers, magazines, radio, television nationally. Traveled extensively to spur recruitment activities on state and local level; extensive liaison work with federal agencies.

(Continued)

Gail R. Geltzer

Bridgeport University—Public Relations, School of Nursing
1963–1966

As branch officer of Bridgeport Information Bureau, planned and directed student recruitment program.
Wrote, placed news and feature stories; produced recruitment literature; established contacts with prospective students, faculty, guidance personnel, alumnae. Responsible for fund-raising activities for an endowed
university chair in nursing.

New York's Children's Hospital—Assistant to Director of Public Relations
1957–1961

Presented stories of services, achievements, needs of hospital, working with newspapers, magazines, radio,
television, educational films. Wrote, produced bimonthly staff house organ and semiannual magazine for
contributors. Devloped and wrote handbooks, pamphlets for patients, staff, donors, nursing school applicants and nursing staff. Assisted staff in preparing manuscripts for professional publications. Helped plan
special events, tours.

Professional Memberships

American Association of Writers, East Coast Chapter; New York Public Relations Association.

Education

M.A., Political Science, Cornell University
B.A., Journalism, Queens College

References: Upon request

IRENE C. NEWMEYER

HOME ADDRESS: 84-84 Dalny Road • Jamaica, New York 11432 • (718) 523-1904

SCHOOL ADDRESS: 4309 Hortensia Avenue • San Diego, California 92130 • (714) 297-9952

JOB OBJECTIVE	A position offering challenge and responsibility in consumer affairs, marketing, or advertising research.
EDUCATION	THE UNIVERSITY OF CALIFORNIA

1985–1989   Graduating in May 1989 with a B.A. Degree in MARKETING AND CONSUMER BEHAVIOR. DEAN'S LIST DISTINCTION.

Field of study includes: marketing and advertising theory and research, economics, business law, calculus, mass communications, statistics, psychology, sociology, and research methodology.

BERKELEY COURSES: Social and Managerial Concepts in Marketing, Consumer Behavior, Product Policy, Advertising Theory and Policies, Sales Force Management, Marketing Research.

SENIOR RESEARCH SEMINARS AND PROJECTS:
- Children and Advertising
- Marketing Research—Cash vs. Credit Retail Analysis
- Portrayal of Women in Magazine Advertising (Role Model)
- Persuasive Impact of Liquor Ads in Print Media
- The Male Contraceptive Pill: Product Development and Marketing Strategies, including Advertising
- Independent study on advertising effectiveness

WORK EXPERIENCE Summers 1988

CALIFDATA CORPORATION—San Diego, California
Administrative assistant in Sales Department. Trained in basic sales and organizational procedures. Responsible for record keeping, expense reports, public relations, correspondence, inventory updates, and billing.

1987   GRAHAM MILLS—La Jolla, California
Basic sales and management training. Responsible for billing, orders, inventory maintenance, shipping arrangements, deliveries.

1986   THE PRESS CLUB (Office)—San Diego, California
Extensive experience in inventory control, contracts, billing, correspondence and public relations.

EXTRA-CURRICULAR ACTIVITIES

Down South—responsible for soliciting advertising as well as writing copy and layout for "Intro to California."
Active with Freshman Orientation Programs. UCSD Marketing and Management Club—involved with structuring innovative lecture series in career opportunities in related fields and designing community "Intern" Program. California Consumer Board—Volunteer.

REFERENCES   Available on request.

HOWARD K. DONALDSON
1170 East Sycamore Lane
Nashville, Tennessee 37204
(615) LO-3-5341

EXPERIENCE:

11/89-present   **NBC News Election Unit**, 30 Tyson Plaza, Atlanta, Georgia.

Work on a free-lance basis assisting in the process of public
opinion polling.
Wrote reports for management on the administration of the polling
operation.

Prior to 1989   **M & M Pharmacy**, 191 Spruce Street, Atlanta, Georgia.

Worked in all phases of neighborhood retail pharmacy except professional services for a period of nine years on both a part-time
basis during the school year and full-time basis during the summer.

Summer 1988   Volunteer work at the South Side Legislative Service Center for
Assemblyman Tyson. Duties included handling constituent prob-
lems, with heavy emphasis on writing correspondence and knowledge of city and state agency functions.

EDUCATION:

1987-1989   **Richmond College**, Richmond, Virginia.

Awarded B.A. in Political Science with Honors in January 1989.

In 1974, participated in Georgia State Assembly Internship Program as a legislative research assistant in the office of then Deputy
Minority Leader John Tyson.

Participated in Atlanta Government Internship Program working in
the office of Councilman Thomas Sample.

1985-1987   **University of Georgia**, Atlanta, Georgia.

References will be furnished upon request.

Paul R. Joseph
2803 Chesapeake ST., NW
Washington, D.C.   10008
(202) 345-9876

Employment <u>Objective</u>

To manage dinner-trade continental restaurant in a suburban setting.

Employment <u>Record</u>

1973-present   Green Door Restaurant, Silver Springs, Md.
                   <u>Assistant Manager</u> to owner-manager. Supervise kitchen, dining and
                   bar staff of 35. Approve menus, maintain food and linen stocks.
                   Initiated wine listing and cellar.

1969-1973   Eight O' Clock Cafes, Washington, D C., Virginia and Maryland.
                   <u>Assistant Quality Control Director</u> for cafe chain. Assessed and main-
                   tained performance standards at seven (originally three) breakfast
                   cafes: food, service, etc. Prepared reports and made recommendations
                   for improvements.

1966-1968   Red Clock Luncheonette, Baltimore, Md.
                   <u>Lunchtime Manager</u>. Supervised lunchtime trade at busy neighbor-
                   hood-type restaurant; filled in as cook, as needed. Maintained receipts.

1962-1966   Rose's Inn, Elkton, Md. <u>Cook</u>. Prepared American/Continental meals
                   in small, family-type restaurant.

Education

  Completed two years at University of Maryland, Accounting major.
  Northeast High School, Baltimore, Md.—Academic Diploma, 1962.

References   Available upon request.

Cheryl Newman
1231 Orchid Street
Los Angeles, California 90068
Phone: (213) 989-2406

JOB OBJECTIVE

Management of American/Continental restaurant in Greater Los Angeles area.

EXPERIENCE

June 1970 –   The French Chef
Present

Assistant Manager — General food service and managerial assistance in this eighty table restaurant. Oversee luncheon and dinner kitchen and dining staffs. Maintain wine and food stocks. Have developed novel seasonal menus in consultation with chef, which have significantly increased volume of business.

September 1968 –   The Oasis Hotel
May 1970

Assistant Banquet Manager — Responsibility for planning and coordination of 100 banquets and private parties per year for from 10-500 guests (business meetings, personal celebrations, community events). Meal planning and "theme" development in consultation with banquet hosts.

June 1966 –
September 1968

Waitress and **Cashier** at the Oasis Hotel, in both luncheonette and formal dining room.

EDUCATION

1971 Successful completion of Restaurant Management course, offered by
      Restaurant Associates of the United States, Inc., Los Angeles, California

1967 A.S. in Food Services, Dallas Junior College, Dallas, Texas

1965 Commercial diploma, Dallas Vocational High School, Dallas, Texas

OTHER ACTIVITIES

Vice Chairman, Los Angeles Restaurant Council

Chairman, Committee for Neighborhood Development, Los Angeles Chamber of Commerce

REFERENCES

Available upon request

Jeremy Gibbons
186 Intracostal Highway
Boca Raton, Florida 33448
(305) 965-9328

Ten years' professional experience in engineering salesmanship.

OBJECTIVE: To serve initially in sales engineering
capacity (sophisticated mechanical equipment)
and ultimately enhance responsibilities
toward engineering management.

EXPERIENCE

Senior
Consultant

The Southern Sun Inc., Boca Raton, Florida - 1984-date.
This position involves the professional selection and sales
of real estate investments, requiring knowledge of tax laws
and shelters as well as applicable real estate laws and
geographical growth trends.

Sales
Engineer

Hobart Air Compressor Corporation, Highland Beach, Florida -
1982-1984.
This position required the sales of industrial air compressors
and their intrinsic components. These components included
regulating, drive, and air drying systems and their auxiliary
support accessories. As technical salesman, incorporated
the attributes of an applicable engineer, sales representative and a field service engineer. A successful sale required the paralleling of stipulated specifications with the
most reliable, effective and economical systems. Frequently
assisted with engineering, assembling, and authoring of
facility expansion or new plant construction specifications.
Often, the installation of new equipment demanded the coordination, instruction, and supervision of mechanical and electrical contractors. Subsequent start-up and troubleshooting
required the establishment of a working relationship with
plant and maintenance personnel.

Student
Trainee

Miami Naval Laboratories, Miami, Florida - 1978-1982.
In conjunction with five year cooperative program, participated in developing, assembling, plotting, and recording
data while working with engineers in the research and
development of shipboard fire fighting systems, high strength
steels and titanium for submarine hulls, and damping materials
for sonar dome application.

(Continued)

EDUCATION

Miami University, Miami, Florida - Mechanical Engineering
B.M.E. June 1978 (Dean's List).

AFFILIATIONS and
LICENSES

Associate Member - American Society of Mechanical Engineers,
F.A.A. Airframe Mechanics License, Florida Teaching
Credential, Florida Real Estate Association.

References furnished upon request.

CLAUDIA MORESCO
80 Central Park West
New York, New York 10014

212-349-1138

RÉSUMÉ CAPSULE   Major career achievements and satisfactions have
                  come from positions with responsibility for the
                  identification and resolution of problems. Skilled
                  in decision-making, including the organization
                  and analysis of data, evaluation of alternative
                  solutions, selection of the optimal approach,
                  and negotiation for the implementation of the
                  decision. Experience in both line and staff
                  positions and strong interpersonal skills.
                  Results-oriented, learn quickly, and enjoy
                  challenge. Accomplishments in all positions are
                  substantiated by rapid salary growth.

EXPERIENCE

July, 1972-   Manager, Academic Market Development, Book and
Present   Information Services, Walton and Champion Companies,
                  Walton, New York. Sales analysis and strategic
                  planning for existing academic market (college and
                  university libraries). New product development
                  including market research, evaluation of external
                  new ventures proposals, initiation of new products
                  and services, financial analyses, and design of
                  marketing offer. Exploration and recommendation
                  of new market segmentation, development of marketing
                  strategies for these segments, preparation of
                  financial projections, and implementation of accepted
                  proposals.

June, 1969-   Gift and Exchange Librarian, Barnard Libraries,
June, 1972   Rochester, New York. Establishment of a department
                  to administer the acceptance and review of gifts
                  to the University libraries. Preparation of a
                  uniform gift policy and procedure manual for ten
                  campus libraries. Negotiation and administration
                  of the exchange of materials with foreign libraries,
                  particularly in the Soviet Union and Latin America.
                  Negotiation with dealers for the sale of unneeded
                  material. Supervision of ten employees.

(Continued)

EDUCATION

M.S.L.S., DeWitt University, January 1971.
M.A.T., Manchester University, June 1967 - Majors: History and Education.

HONORS

Dean's List all semesters
Phi Beta Kappa
Beta Phi Mu honorary

References

Available upon request

June Brown
30 Broad Street
Atlanta, Georgia   30397
(404) 821-5994

Job Objective: A responsible and challenging opportunity
                        in the administrative area of sales.

Experience:
1971-present   National Accounts Manager, Beautiful
                        Hair and Cosmetics, Inc., Atlanta,
                        Georgia
                        Responsible for a $6 million sales volume
                        in territory east of Mississippi includ-
                        ing hiring and training all new sales
                        personnel, supervising and coordinating
                        activities of all Manufacturers' Repre-
                        sentatives; have increased sale volume
                        30% since April 1976.

Education:
1967-1971   B.A. - University of Georgia

References: Appropriate references will be submitted
                        upon request.

Edward Salson
144-30 Ford Brooks Road
Citadel, California 95610

business
experience

October 1985–
March 1989

Gibson Color Systems, Hudson, New Hampshire

Offset preparatory firm located in New Hampshire with a New York Sales Office.

Salesperson—Developing and servicing accounts handled out of the New York area. Estimated cost of preparatory work including separating and stripping job into position. Handling color correcting press proofs and detail work pertaining to a given job.

December 1978–
September 1985

Shank Graphics, Chicago, Illinois

Litho and Gravure separator with a St. Paul Office.

Sales and Sales Service—Responsibilities included servicing established accounts and opening up new accounts. Did all the estimating for the St. Paul office.

February 1976–
December 1978

Baronet Litho Company, Jamestown, Virginia

Small commercial printer. Equipment included a 60-inch four-color press. Plant had complete facilities including stripping, platemaking and bindery and mailing department.

Assistant to Plant Manager—Handled all jobs received from salespeople. Made out job tickets and job layouts. Followed through on all jobs in various stages of production. Ordered paper and other items necessary to produce final product.

education

Rochester Institute of Technology

Earned B.S. in General Printing, 1976
Earned A.A.S. degree in Photographic Science, 1974

references

Will be furnished upon request.

GREGG D. LEWIS
1085 WARBURTON AVENUE, APARTMENT 808
YONKERS, NEW YORK   10701
914/423-5858

EXPERIENCE

MILLER PRODUCTS, DIVISION OF   MAY 1984 TO PRESENT
MILLER-WALLER, INC.

Sales Promotion Manager

   Coordinate promotions for brand and sales management.
   Includes: budgeting, planning, creative and complete implementations of plans.

   Manage department of four. Responsibilities for all
   sales promotional materials: artwork, printing, displays,
   premiums, sampling and couponing.

   Negotiate for services of mailing and sampling executions,
   fulfillment houses, and coupon clearing organizations.

   Successfully introduced Dri XX Spray, Dri XX Roll On
   Deodorant and Dew Drops with Fluoride: developed and
   executed promotion plan and strategy.

   Promotion budget of $10 million.

BEAUTIFUL HAIR, INC.   FEBRUARY 1982 TO MAY 1984

Product Promotion Manager

   Responsible for all retail promotion programs in the Hair
   Color and Toiletries Division: trade promotions, collateral
   material, pricing, sales objectives, and advertising plans
   by sales region.

   Developed promotion plans and executed them for new products:
   trade strategy, sampling, couponing, ad sales materials.
   New products include Essence Shampoo that grew to number
   three in shampoo market.

   Worked closely with research, production planning, legal,
   graphic suppliers, and ad agency.

   Promotion budget of $12 million.

   Heavy business travel.

Assistant Product Promotion Manager

Assisted the position "Production Promotion Manager" in all areas
explained.

(Continued)

Sales Representative　　　　　　　　　　　　JANUARY 1978 TO FEBRUARY 1982

Managed merchandise shows for company in local markets. Responsibility for sales volume in 150 direct and indirect accounts. Worked closely with company research in new product tests including: implementation of new product sales plans, weekly audits and test analysis.

EDUCATION

University of North Carolina, 1978
B.S. in Business Administration/Marketing

REFERENCES

Available upon request.

ALBERTO ROSSI
One Top Stone Drive
Toledo, Ohio 43614
(419) 361-7444

EDUCATION

B.S. degree, Business Administration; Marketing Major, University of California, Northridge - 1968

EXPERIENCE

HIGHLY VISIBLE SOFTWARE CO., Toledo, Ohio

12/82 to Present   **National Account Manager**

Sell a variety of software to run on UNIX-based workstations, including Electronic Mail and Word Processing packages. Received 4 top sales awards; 1 of 2 salesmen in company to receive sales award for exceeding $2M in sales.

CREATIVE SOFTWARE, Los Angeles, California

6/81 to 12/82   **Regional Marketing Manager**

Responsible for all sales, marketing, staffing, and budgeting activity for four branch offices located within southern California, Arizona, and Colorado. Other activities included sales training, product positioning, product exposure, selling methodology, and sales manual development.

CSI/TEKNITRON, Greensboro, North Carolina

1971 to 1981   **Major Account Manager**

Marketing activity included direct sales to Fortune 1000 and California 100 companies. Succeeded in selling and installing over 150 CSI Data Processing Systems, qualifying me for numerous "100% Clubs." Involved in other projects such as competitive analysis, sales training, and sales compensation.

DELTA/MICROFILM BUSINESS SYSTEMS, Durham, North Carolina

1968 to 1970   **National Sales Manager**

Established a national sales organization to market computer output microfilm services. Responsible for all direct sales activity, sales training, and development of marketing policy.

PERSONAL

Willing to relocate

References available upon request

Khanh Van Chen
488-1/2 State Street
San Francisco, California 94063
(415) 555-2345

Five years' professional and educational experience in counseling.

OBJECTIVE: To augment professional placement service
by contributing expertise in interviewing,
personnel, and guidance counseling.

AMPLIFICATION: To serve organization in private industry
and ultimately develop skills for managerial
position.

EXPERIENCE

Program
Coordinator

San Francisco Manpower Corporation, San Francisco, California - 1984 to date
This position involves the coordination of six dissimilar
office skill training programs encompassing paraprofessional
and professional personnel. As program coordinator and
senior counselor, supervise thirty-four staff members and
one hundred thirty trainees for each rotating cycle.
Frequently instrumental in placing graduating trainees to
applicable jobs and training them accordingly. Utilize
public relations skills during heavy telephone work in
contacting and solidifying prospective employers.

Publishing
Secretary

Santana Publishing Company, San Francisco, California -
1983 to 1984
This position required the screening and interpreting of
telephone calls, written and oral communications concerning
inter-office memorandums, and correspondences between
management and accounting staff personnel.

Graduate
Assistant

University of Nebraska, Smokeville, Nebraska - 1982-1983
In conjunction with work-study tuition program, arranged
class schedules for students. Counseled foreign students
with their academic, social, language adjustment, family,
and immigration problems by applying principles of guidance.

EDUCATION

University of Nebraska, Smokeville, Nebraska - M.Ed., 1983
Major: Guidance and Counseling

University of Taiwan, Taiwan - B.A., 1982
Major: English

(Continued)

SPECIAL AWARDS

Scholarship to attend world-wide guidance and counseling
convention. Coordinator of foreign students workshop.
Champion debator, third year, college.

PUBLICATIONS

Editor - newsletter and brochure for San Francisco Manpower
Corporation.

REFERENCES

Available upon request.

CHARLOTTE KEANE
14 Wateview St.
Silver Springs, MD 41814
(301) 899-9248
(301) 791-2300

CAREER OBJECTIVE:

To work exclusively for a designer in a showroom presenting that designer's line to retail clothing buyers.

BUSINESS EXPERIENCE:

5/87–5/88   PEGGY LANE & Co.
Washington, DC

Assistant manager for junior sportswear.
Interviewed, trained, and supervised all new employees. Responsible for designing and implementing the weekly displays.

6/86–9/86   McGRAW'S
Washington, DC

Manager of restaurant and amusement complex.
Designed menu, hired employees, worked with decorators to create proper ambiance in restaurant, managed inventories, controlled
cash flow and budgets, and supervised all employees. $250,000 gross receipts during summer months.

6/85–9/85   CLASSIC CLOTHES
Bethesda, MD

Sales associate. Provided fashion consulting and helped to create window and store displays.

EDUCATION:

1986–1988   UNIVERSITY OF CONNECTICUT

BS Degree Fashion Merchandising (May 1988)
Member of Omicron Nu Honor Society

1983–1985   MARYMOUNT UNIVERSITY
Arlington, VA
Dean's List. President of Resident Dormitory

PERSONAL BACKGROUND:

Traveled in parts of Europe and the United States.

REFERENCES:

Provided upon request.

Dorothy Turner
415 Oakes Street
St. Paul, Minnesota   55149
(612) 654-1234

Experience

April 1985-
present

<u>Medical Caseworker</u>, Catholic Churches, St. Paul,
Minnesota. Interview patients and their families
at St. Claire's Hospital to ascertain needs of
home care; arrange for volunteer nursing and
housekeeping and child care assistance.

June 1975-
March 1985

<u>Family Caseworker</u>, K.H. Psychiatric Clinic,
St. Paul, Minnesota. Conducted therapy sessions
for teenagers, adults and children; interviewed
families of patients to determine financial
competency and arranged for financial help.

Education

1975

M.S.W. - Columbia School of Social Work,
New York City

1974

B.A. - University of Minnesota, St. Paul,
Minnesota

References

Available upon request.

Adrienne Smithfield
22 Olive Tree Street
Kansas City, Missouri 64116

(816) 546-9865

EXPERIENCE

1970–present   **Children's Caseworker, Angel of Mercy Home.** Kansas City, Mo. Interview children and families of children at Angel of Mercy Home. The home takes both orphans and children from inadequate homes. Do full investigations. Follow up. Make recommendations concerning children.

1968–1970   **Family Caseworker, Kansas City State Hospital.** Interviewed members of families at the hospital or at their homes. Helped to make for better adjustment. Proposed plans for assisting patients.

EDUCATION

B.S., Social Work, Southern Missouri State College, Springfield, Missouri. Concentrated training in social work with an emphasis on psychiatric and pediatric.

PROFESSIONAL AFFILIATIONS

National Association of Social Workers and National Caseworkers Ass'n.

REFERENCES

References covering all phases of education and experience on request.

William Fredericks
314 San Fernando Avenue
Hohokus, New Jersey 07423   Telephone: (201) 456-4921

Job Objective: To obtain a position in a field where past supervisory
                experience may eventually be utilized.

Past Experience
1985 to present   Winkler, Cantor and Pomboy (Investments),
                              N.Y., N.Y. (Experience similar to that stated
                              for D.H. Blair and Co.)

1978 to 1984   **As Supervisor**, responsible for entire work output
D.H. Blair and Co.   and efficiency of Order Room; proper execution
(Investments) N.Y., N.Y.   of orders for brokers, banks and institutional
                              funds; assisted brokers in general operations;
                              served as liaison with other brokerage firms on
                              daily transactions and problems. Position required
                              knowledge of stock exchange operations, figure
                              aptitude, decision-making and absolute accuracy
                              under extreme pressure.

1972 to 1978   **Senior Order Clerk** and supervisor of branch
                              office of Tessel, Paturick and Ostrau, Inc.
                              (Investments) N.Y., N.Y.

1960 to 1972   **Cashier** with Merrill, Lynch, Pierce, Fenner and
                              Smith, N.Y., N.Y. - handled large volumes of cash
                              and securities; was bonded; supervised three
                              cashier clerks; trained approximately 25 broker
                              trainees in all phases of backstage branch opera-
                              tions.

Education: Special Schools: Finance Institutes for
                                                special courses in connec-
                                                tion with banking and
                                                brokerage operations--1960.

References: Available upon request.

CLYDE HENLEY
P.O. Box 92
Cranberry Lake, NJ 08540
609-346-1130

RESUME CAPSULE: Twenty years' experience as Industrial Foreman,
with superior mechanical ability, production
efficiency, leadership and excellent record in
labor relations.

EXPERIENCE

1968-present   Foreman, Ginger Beverages Company, Marshall,
New Hampshire. One of the largest manufacturers of ginger beverages and crystallized
ginger products in the United States. Supervise work of eighteen employees operating
ginger presses, pulverizers, and separators,
producing four varieties of ginger flavored
beverages and confections. Full responsibility
of hiring and supervising employees, training
operators, and establishing work hours and
shifts. Excellent rapport with employees
resulting in minimal grievances with union.

1966-1968   Foreman, Spartan Separators, Inc., Madison,
N.J. One of America's major manufacturers
of separating equipment for use in food processing. Worked in machine assembly department
as night supervisor with full responsibility
for faultless assembly of food processing
equipment.

1962-1966   Tool and Die Maker, Waterford Machine Production Company. Suggested design modifications,
kept production moving. Worked as assistant
night superintendent during rush periods.

EDUCATION

Graduate Brooklawn High School, Brooklawn, N.J. - 1962.
(Mechanical)

REFERENCES

Upon request.

Mary Conklin Rogers
57 Lee Avenue
Columbus, Ohio 42317
Home phone: (614) 456-2397
Business phone: (614) 675-9000

Experience

1977 to present

Receptionist/Switchboard Operator

Pathway Employment Agency, Columbus, Ohio.
Responsibilities include operating busy 555
board, greeting job applicants and clients,
administering and grading typing tests,
filing and assisting in mailings.

1972 to 1977

Receptionist

Regal Paper Company, Columbus, Ohio.
Handled busy monitor board, and all
bookkeeping including accounts
receivable.

Education

Commerce High School,Columbus, Ohio.
Commercial Diploma. Graduated June,
1972.

References

Available upon request.

Kevin J. Hutchins
69 Marrietta Drive
Dallas, Texas 75234

Telephone: (214) 459-9345

Job Objective: Systems Analyst

Experience

1974- present	Programmer Supervisor Hartman Oil Company Dallas, Texas

Writes computer programs, developing block diagrams,
utilizing available software and operating systems, and
coding machine instructions. Originates block diagrams,
working from outlines of proposed systems, develops file
sizes, programming specifications. Determines appropriate
use of tape or disk files, printer, etc. Selects in-house
software or sub-routines to run in connection with program.

Writes machine instructions, tests, debugs, and assembles
program. Documents overall system and develops data control
procedures. Advises and instructs less experienced programmers and prepares operating instructions.

1970-1974	Programmer Live Oak Electronics Houston, Texas

As a trainee for six months, became proficient in COBOL
programming. Coded well-defined systems logic flow charts
into computer machine instructions using COBOL. Coded sub-
routines following specifications, file size parameters,
block diagrams. Performed maintenance tasks and patching
to established, straightforward programs. Documented all
programs as completed. Tested, debugged and assembled programs.

Education   Levitt High School, Temple, Texas - Graduated 1968.

Houston Community College - 1968-1970. Completed two-year course.

References   Provided on request.

ROSETTA BROWN
55 Atlanta Avenue
Roselle, New York   14512

716-366-9032

EXPERIENCE

1972–present	Elementary Teacher, Greendale Public Schools, Greendale, New York. Taught fourth and fifth grades. Complete responsibility for the writing, reading and research for a Teacher's Kit-Children's Literature. (A synopsis, discussion questions and enrichment multi-media activities for over 55 outstanding children's novels.)
1968–1972	Elementary Teacher, Greendale Public Schools, Greendale, New York. Taught second and third grades. Participated in much curriculum work, area of upgraded classes and inter-age grouping.
1967–1968	Receptionist, Robinson and Sons, New York City.
1966–1967	Saleswoman, The Tog Shop, New York City.
1965–1966	Reservationist, Landover Air Lines, New York, N.Y.

EDUCATION

M.A., June 1968–Adelphi University. Elementary Education.

Permanent Certification, 1967.
Common Branch Subjects (1–6)
The Universtiy of the State of New York.

B.A., June 1965–Russell College. English Major.

REFERENCES

Will be furnished upon request.

ALYSON REXDALE
60 West End Avenue
New York, N.Y. 10023

(212) 866-5332

EXPERIENCE

1985-present   Teacher, Stuyvesant Elementary School, Rochester, New York. Took into account long range goals of individual students as well as class as a unit, and developed and organized unit in consumer education utilizing visual and audio media. Created and developed working models for use of children to promote coordination and mental stimulation.

1981-1982   Tutored German children in English while at a German University in Stuttgart on Exchange Study Program.

EDUCATION

M.S., Elementary Education, Brampton College, Rochester, N.Y. 1985.

New York State Teacher's Certificate (N-6) #489664101, effective September, 1985.

B.A., Psychology. State University of New York at Albany, 1983.

SPECIAL RECOGNITION

New York State Regents Scholarship—1979-1983

REFERENCES

Will be furnished upon request.

Robert R. Abbey
48 Mingus Circle
Bayonne, New Jersey   07002

OBJECTIVE: Appointment on teaching staff of small private
                 institution in rural area, preferably in
                 New York State.

EXPERIENCE:

April 1974-   Teacher/Instructor in Charge of Training and
Present   Development, Eastern Academy, Fort Lee,
                 New Jersey.

September 1973- Assistant Dean of Students, Parkwood Junior
March 1974   College, Parkwood, New Hampshire. In charge
                 of all student personnel programs, including
                 Career Counseling, Job Placement, Student
                 Government, Admissions Recruitment, Discipline,
                 Athletics, Cultural Development, and Student
                 Welfare Benefits.

September 1971- Instructor, Glendale High School, Glendale,
June 1973   N.Y. Taught basic Art Courses and American
                 History.

EDUCATIONAL
BACKGROUND

M.A. (History/English), 1971 - Wayne University, Michigan.

B.S. Education (History), 1970 - St. Michael's College,
New Jersey.

REFERENCES will be furnished upon request.

MARTHA KAYE
16 Court St.
Chicago, IL 24168

(213) 841-1286
(213) 911-4000

EXPERIENCE

November 1984
to
June 1988

Accepted a position with Valley & Williams & Co., Inc, established in to 1879, one of the oldest and most prestigious New City travel agencies. Responsibilities encompassed counseling for FIT cruise and land travel arrangements, plus preparation of itineraries, tickets, and necessary travel documents. Raymond & Whitcomb sponsors cruise programs for cultural organizations and promotes allotments for Royal Viking Line and Windstar Cruises. The agency arranges cruise and land programs for the Metropolitan Museum of Art, The Chicago Art Institute, the Smithsonian, the Brooklyn Botanical Garden and others. During my tenure I was responsible for various departures—including selling and document processing. Raymond & Whitcomb utilizes PARS airline computer, Digital Word Processing, and ITT telex.

January 1963
to
October 1984

Owned and managed Sante Travel Agency, St. Louis, Missouri. Sante Travel Agency is a prestigious St. Louis agency with a staff of fifteen and sales in excess of three million. During this time in the travel industry, I successfully marketed domestic and international tours, wrote brochures, conducted tour groups, sold cruises, charters, and consulted with St. Louis cultural organizations for specialized sponsored tours: the Zoo, Art Museum, and Missouri Botanical Garden. I maintained a working knowledge of computers, agency business practices, cost and profitability factors. I planned and processed FIT travel arrangements for clients to every part of the world. I have travelled extensively world-wide, and I have a personal knowledge of touring and hotel facilities in the following countries: United States, England, Scotland, France, Germany, Italy, Portugal, New Zealand, Australia, New Guinea, China, Yugoslavia, Indonesia, Egypt, India, South America, South and East Africa, Scandinavia, Russia, Greece, Morocco, Israel, and the Caribbean. Sante Travel Agency utilized Sabre airline computer system.

EDUCATION

1987 Completed ICTA course and received certification as a CTC.

1959-1963 Washington University, St. Louis, B.A. degree.

1959 Graduated Mary Institute, a St. Louis girls preparatory day school.

REFERENCES

To be furnished on request.

Lindsay Marie Wells
3546 Swarr Run Road
Lancaster, Pennsylvania 17603
(717) 955-2937

EXPERIENCE:

May 1972-
present

NATIONAL INSTITUTE OF CERTIFIED PUBLIC ACCOUNTANTS
Manager, Salary Administration - Responsible for administration of salary increase program including promotional increases, adjustments, monthly merit increase reviews, performance appraisal program and job evaluation. Conducting compensation surveys to determine necessity of adjusting exempt and non-exempt salary ranges. Participating in various compensation surveys. Maintaining employee budget. Developing and revising policies and procedures. Counseling employees. Advising personnel employees on job-related problems. Administration and supervision of personnel department in Director's absence.

January 1971-
May 1972

BOOKER AND BOOKER
Personnel Assistant - Responsible for smooth running of personnel; function on a day-to-day basis included interviewing and hiring of administrative staff, obtaining temporary personnel, supervising work-study employees, and keeping personnel records. Prepared and filed various governmental reports including Veteran Reports. Processed some benefits claims and administered the salary increase program.

June 1967-
December 1969

WATERMAN HOUSE, INC.
Wage and Salary Specialist - Responsible for maintaining an equitable salary administration program, including meeting with department managers in order to study and analyze jobs, preparation of job descriptions, evaluation of jobs using established system to determine grades and prepare records of validity. Developed new evaluation system for exempt and non-exempt employees, Prepared and maintained merit increase budget and rate schedules, and organization charts and listings for all divisions.

EDUCATION:

1965-1967   Pitt Community College - A.A. Degree (Psychology).

1971-1974   Various AMA and Commerce and Industry Courses dealing with Personnel.

REFERENCES: Available upon request.

Sylvia Martinson
16 Beverly Place
Los Angeles, CA 41825
(519) 845-7633

BUSINESS EXPERIENCE:

4/87–Present

Word Processor
Career Blazers
Temporary Personnel
Los Angeles, CA

Word Processor
Career Blazers
Temporary Personnel
White Plains, NY

2/82–3/87

Word Processor
B.B. & K. Sales, Inc.
Brooklyn, NY

Word Processor
Duties include typing contracts, reviewing title searches, contacting clients for timely return of documents, scheduling dates for closing with parties and attorneys, accepting binders determining prospective clients' eligibillty, preparing contractors' worksheets, making judgements as to what repairs needed immediate attention before property could be made available for sale or rent, proofreading and editing contracts, manuscripts and correspondence. Extensive use of IBM-PC utilizing MultiMate and WordPerfect.

3/77–1/82

Baker & Ross, Inc.
Brooklyn, NY

Administrative Assistant
Duties include reviewing tenants' files, conducting recertification of tenants' eligibility to determine rate of rent, verifying prospective tenants' living quarters, maintaining log of payments, payments past due and supervising the repairs of apartments and the building in general.

EDUCATION:

9/86–Present

New York Technical College.
Associates degree. Major in Liberal Arts.

6/68–6/72

Thomas Jefferson High School, Academic degree.

SKILLS:

Typing: 65 wpm
IBM/PC, AT and XT
IBM Selectric II
WordStar, OfficeWriter, MultiMate, WordPerfect, Wang,
Diagram Master, MultiPlan

REFERENCES:

Furnished upon request.

Dorothy Turner
415 Oakes Street
St. Paul, Minnesota 55149
(612) 654-1234

Objective   Secure a position as a technical writer.

Education   M.A. (English), University of Illinois, 1983
                   B.S. (Education), University of Illinois, 1982

Experience   St. Paul High School   1988-1989
                   High School English Teacher

                   Responsible for teaching English (writing,
                   grammar, and literature) and history in secondary
                   school.

                   Geigo Terminal Systems, Minneapolis, Minn.
                                                           1985-1988
                   Senior Technical Editor (1986-1988)

                   Responsible for editing user manuals, programming
                   guides, and feature summaries for Geigo terminals
                   and related computer equipment.

                   Additionally responsible for the quality control
                   of technical documentation; assisted writers with
                   writing and editing problems, and instructed
                   writers individually and in seminars; also on-call
                   to edit other corporation documents.

                   Instrumental in providing the company with
                   accuracy, precision, and consistency in
                   documentation by researching, compiling, and
                   editing a glossary of standard terms used by Geigo
                   in reference to its products. (This glossary and
                   my guidelines for technical writing are still used
                   by Geigo.)

                   Software Technical Writer (1985-1986)

                   Responsible for researching, writing, and
                   producing system operation and programming guides,
                   and feature summaries; assisted in designing the
                   documents from inception through production.
                   Interfaced with engineering, marketing, and
                   graphic arts.

(Continued)

Freelance Writer and Consultant   1984-1985

Employed by several computer and publishing firms,
as follows:

C.B.S. Data Corporation -- Wrote abstracts of
articles from commercial banking publications;
wrote critiques of competitors' advertising.

John Wiley & Sons -- Proofread and copyedited
portions of high school texts.

Loeb Publishing -- Wrote exercises for college
grammar text; proofread and copyedited the K-8
reading series.

Kodak Corporation -- Edited scientific articles
and user manuals.

I.E.E.E. -- Proofread and edited hardware and
software documents and textbooks.

Related   Wrote reviews and feature articles for corporation
Experience   newspaper; wrote some advertising copy; wrote a
                   critical biography; wrote courses of study.

                   Conducted workshops and seminars in technical
                   writing and expository composition; chaired
                   committees on curriculum development.

                   Evaluated compositions for College Entrance
                   Examinations Board.

                   Taught grammar and writing in college and adult
                   education.

References   On Request.

Barbara Berkman
47 East 72nd Street
New York, New York 10027

OBJECTIVE   Technical Writer

PROFESSIONAL
ACCOMPLISHMENTS

Software   . Designed and implemented programs in BASIC,
                     ASSEMBLY, and COBOL
                   . Logged 200+ hours on the DEC PDP-11/44
                   . Created text files and source programs
                     using EMACS
                   . Completed course on Wang word processor

Writing   . Completed 200 hours of technical writing
                     instruction
                   . Wrote technical documents:
                     - JCL Reference Manual
                     - EMACS Reference Guide
                   . Designed instructional materials including:
                     - 3 videocassette training aids for
                       welfare workers
                     - course syllabus with 30 content units
                     - more than 30 course handouts
                     - 2 chapters of an instructional booklet
                     - evaluation questionnaires

Training   . Prepared and delivered training program to
                     clerical staff of NY State Welfare Department
                   . Designed and delivered classroom lectures
                   . Trained and supervised instructional staff
                     of 15
                   . Utilized a wide variety of audiovisual equip-
                     ment including films, slides, overheads,
                     videocassettes, and slide tapes
                   . Performed needs analyses and implemented
                     programs based on results of analyses

Management   . Acted as department coordinator; supervised
                     faculty
                   . Interviewed, evaluated, and recommended candi-
                     dates for university faculty positions
                   . Negotiated learner contracts at community
                     agencies
                   . Chaired Course Development Committee
                   . Coordinated social services to a diverse
                     community population

(Continued)

EDUCATION	. Technical Writing Program, Brooklyn Community College, 1988 . Personnel Development: Design of Training Programs, Hofstra University, 1981 . M.S. in Social Work, Hofstra University, 1980, GPA 3.9 . B.S. in English, SUNY, Stony Brook, 1968, Magna Cum Laude
EXPERIENCE	. Staff Social Worker. St. Joseph's Hospital, Long Island, N.Y. 1981-1986 . Instructor, Parent Education. St. Joseph's Hospital, Long Island, N.Y. 1978-1983 . Assistant Professor, School of Social Services. Long Island University, 1975-1981 . Social Worker, N.Y. State Social Services Program, New York, New York. 1970-1974 . Social Worker, St. Joseph's Hospital, Long Island, N.Y. 1968-1970
PROFESSIONAL ORGANIZATION	Society for Technical Communication
REFERENCES	References and writing sample available upon request

Which Job Do I Take?

You've spent weeks on the hunt and you've bagged your quarry: two or three job offers. Now you have a new problem: your thoughts change from "How do I get the job I want?" to "Which one shall I accept?" What? You think that's an easy decision and that you'd take the job that offers the most money? Well, maybe yes, and maybe no. There's more to be considered than just money.

Say you're a recent college graduate and you never worked fulltime before. You've come to a large metopolis because you know that's where your future lies. You don't know *anybody*. After weeks of searching you have had two job offers. In one, the higher paid of the two, you will be working in a small office with one or two other people; in the other, with five percent less pay, you'll be a member of a large staff and will have the opportunity to meet lots of people.

Since you've come to the city to start a whole new life, you must consider that a job that offers an opportunity to expand your social life might offer something as valuable as money. That is one of the many intangibles you must consider in the job selection process. Here are some others:

Some companies provide training programs; others are willing to pay part (or all) of the costs of specialized university courses for you to add to your skills and knowledge. How valuable is that? What is it worth? What will that additional education be worth in the future? This is another area to consider.

The geographical location of a job should influence your decision. If it would require you to relocate, shoud you? Have you thought about the cost of living in a different city? Remember, to judge the worth of your salary properly, it must be compared to the cost of living. What about cultural activities in the new city? And how important are they to you?

Even without relocation, you must consider the location of your job. Perhaps you are one of those people who seeks some diversion during the lunch hour—visiting a museum or doing some shoppping. A job in the boondocks offering a few dollars more than one close to a cultural or shopping area might not interest you then. One requiring fifteen minutes' travel—a short walk from your home—could be preferable to another with a higher salary and an hour's bus or subway ride away. Often, a slight difference in salary is more than eaten up by transportation costs. Besides, time going to and from work is not exactly leisure time!

Be sure in making your decision that you consider the

importance of being happy with your new job. My agency advises entry-level job seekers to take the job they instinctively feel "good" about. We've found that being happy in a job almost guarantees better job performance and hence promotion. We've also found that most companies promote from within and will always consider their staff members for each new job opportunity. Our philosophy is "Proximity is the mother of opportunity," and, therefore, the "wrong job in the right company" often or usually becomes the "right job in the right company."

A beginner should also consider possibilities in job hunting. Your first job should be considered as a place to learn, to get experience, and to prove yourself.

If you consider everything in your life as a growing experience and give it the best you have, you'll be bringing the ingredient of success to any job you take.

The many intangibles in selecting which job offer to take also apply to every job seeker.

For example, is there a company cafeteria? Many companies have them and offer good, nutritious food to their employees at low cost. Considering that, in many instances, a full meal at the company cafeteria will cost less than a hamburger and beverage at a luncheonette or fast-food counter, you would be able to save. How important would the advantages of this be in terms of economics and convenience? Certainly worth thinking about!

The health plan offered is another important factor. Young people very often tend to disregard a firm's hospital and major medical plans—they even consider themselves both indestructible and immortal! But anyone, of any age, can suddenly find himself or herself confronted with a stay in the hospital, resulting in large medical bills.

If you are married with children, you probably are more aware of the value of a good medical plan, but do you know that some companies offer psychiatric and dental coverage as well? How many parents of a troubled teenager would welcome psychiatric coverage! Perhaps you have a child who will need orthodontia work in two or three years. If, among your job offers, is a company that offers no dental plan at all and another that offers all or a percentage of dental costs, you must weigh carefully just how important such a plan is to you.

If you're an "over-forty" person and expect to stay in this job until your retirement, try to find out which offer will give you the most career advancement. One of the firms that has offered you a job may have the levels above your position filled by people your age or younger. But another firm might be able to offer you a position as soon as the immediate supervisor reaches retirement age. How quickly can you get promoted? How high can you go in the company? These, too, are considerations.

Just as job searching is a thinking process, so is job selection. There's much to think about in selecting which job offer to accept. It is never solved by simply flipping a coin. You must try to really think about *you*, decide what is important to *you*, and in which job *you* think *your* skills, talents, and abilities will be used to the most advantage, and where *you* will be the happiest.

And once you make the decision, stick to it, and commit yourself completely. The job-getting is just the first step. The next achievement is in making the job into *your* job. By giving it your all and approaching it with integrity and imagination, you will change your job into a challenging career.

Index to Model Résumés

The model résumés are organized alphabetically. In some cases there will be several résumés for the same field to show that *every* résumé in a particular field is in itself *unique* and *different*. In other words, each résumé has its singular job descriptions and histories. If you are unable to find a sample résumé fitting your actual job description, model yours after one fitting a similar job title.

Though you refer to the following résumés, never copy them or any parts of them. Your own writing will ring truer if it is completely your own work.

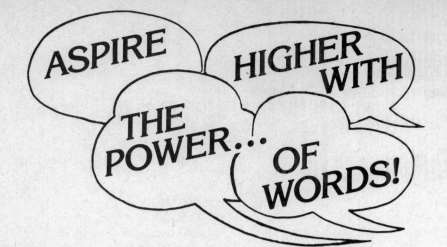

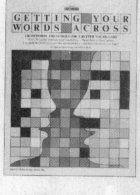
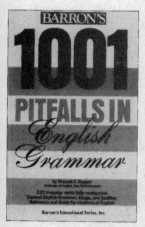
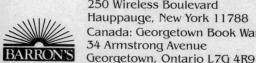